PIE
in the
SKY

PIE

in the

SKY

CURIOUS, BIZARRE AND INCOMPREHENSIBLE
EXPRESSIONS EXPLAINED

This edition published in 2015 by Baker & Taylor UK Ltd.
Bicester.
Oxfordshire

© 2015 Susanna Geoghegan Gift Publishing
Collated and edited by Fiona Thornton
Illustrations by Lorenzo Montatore
Design by Milestone Design
Layout by Bag of Badgers

ISBN 978-1-910562-00-0

Printed in China.

Introduction

Have you ever stopped to wonder where all our quirky everyday sayings come from? We take many of them for granted because they sum up perfectly what we're trying to say – 'a clean bill of health' or 'as the crow flies' are commonly understood, as are 'turning a blind eye' or passing an exam 'with flying colours'. But these, and hundreds more such sayings, have a fascinating history.

In these pages you will find a selection of common expressions, along with explanations of – or admittedly sometimes just theories about – their origin. Did you know, for example, that 'making a bee-line' for somewhere is something that bees actually do? Or that in days gone by it was believed that 'licking into shape' was done literally? Would you be surprised to discover that many of the sayings and metaphors that we use daily stem from Britain's maritime heritage? Or that a good number come from the worlds of horse racing and card playing?

Dip into the pages that follow and all will be revealed. Hopefully by the time you've finished reading you'll feel that you 'know your onions' – and what you've found out will be interesting enough not to send you to 'the land of nod'!

A1

Anything designated 'A1' is recognised these days as being the very best of its kind or top quality. The expression comes from the Lloyd's of London Register of Shipping. The condition of a ship's hull was rated by letters and that of its anchors and other equipment by figures. By this system a ship classified as 'A1' received the highest rating possible and it wasn't long before A1 became a widely used term for 'excellent'.

A lot on your plate

To have 'a lot on your plate' means to feel overloaded with too much to deal with. In polite society, literally having too much food piled high on your plate was a sign of greed. It could also show poor judgement, and you might be accused of having 'eyes bigger than your stomach' when food is left uneaten on the plate.

A watched pot never boils

We all know that time seems to go more slowly when you're waiting for something to happen, and this old domestic saying sums that up nicely. Of course in times gone by, a family meal would often be cooked all in one pot hung over the fire, so the sense of impatience while waiting for the food to cook might have seemed greater. You sometimes also hear 'a watched kettle never boils', but the more efficient modern kettles become, the less apt a metaphor this will be!

ABOVE BOARD

If something is 'above board', it's legal and out in the open. The expression derives from card games, where players were required to keep their hands in sight, above the playing surface, to avoid any accusation of surreptitiously changing cards or cheating in any way. From the same context come 'laying your cards on the table', in other words being open and honest about your intentions, 'showing your hand', meaning disclosing your motives and 'throwing in your hand', meaning giving up.

Above the salt/
Below the salt

Salt probably isn't the first thing that comes to mind as an indication of social standing, but in medieval times, when feasts were held at long tables with a salt cellar in the middle, it was a clear sign of status. Those who sat 'above the salt', i.e. between the salt cellar and the hosts, were of higher social standing than those who had the misfortune to be placed 'below the salt'.

Acid test

Gold remains unaffected by most acids, so its authenticity could be proved with a simple 'acid test' – now of course, the expression has come to mean any process that proves something beyond doubt.

Across the board

Meaning 'generally' or 'applying to everyone', across the board originated in the world of horse racing. A board would be used to display the odds on each horse in a race, and an 'across the board' bet placed odds on a horse coming in first, second or third.

Adam's ale

A light-hearted term for water. 'Adam's ale' refers of course to the biblical story of Adam. who as the first man on earth drank the pure. clean waters of the Garden of Eden. Conversely. the 'demon drink'. otherwise known as alcohol. is associated with the devil. There's an irony here. though – the word 'whisky' comes from the Gaelic 'water of life' and the word 'vodka' can be literally translated as 'little water'!

Against the grain

Something that 'goes against the grain' goes against the natural order of things or the way they should best be done. The phrase has been used since at least the seventeenth century and refers to working with wood. when it is much easier to literally work with the grain than to try and work against it.

All at sea

When you're 'all at sea' you are in a state of uncertainty. or confused about something. Dating from the nineteenth century. the saying is an allusion to a mariner out of sight of land who has lost his bearings and consequently has no idea of his position on the chart.

ALL SHIP-SHAPE AND BRISTOL FASHION

Bristol was once one of Britain's largest ports, and had an enviable reputation for efficiency. So just as a ship, and its port, had to be well organised, so anything that is 'ship-shape and Bristol fashion' is well prepared for an undertaking.

An apple a day keeps the doctor away

These days, we are encouraged to eat far more than just one piece of fruit a day. Nevertheless the nutritional value of certain foods has long been recognised, and it seems from this popular nineteenth-century saying that the humble apple was given especial prominence for its health benefits.

An Englishman's home is his castle

A saying dear to the heart of every Englishman, it was Sir Edward Coke, the Lord Chief Justice from 1613–17, who enshrined the principle in his Institutes, which are considered to be a legal classic. Coke was seen as a great defender of the common law against the right of the Crown and wrote: 'The house of every man is to him as his castle and fortresse, as well as for his defence against injury and violence ...'

In modern times, of course, under certain conditions, a number of public authorities have the right of entry to a private house – and in extreme cases can even destroy it, under the terms of compulsory purchase orders.

Apple-pie bed

With duvets becoming the norm, the making of an apple-pie bed may be a prank that is dying out. Essentially it means folding the bed sheet in two so that when a person tries to slip into bed, they cannot stretch their legs out. However, the phrase actually has nothing to do with apples, or indeed pies, but is a corruption of the French nappe pliée or 'folded cloth'.

From the same source we get the expression 'apple-pie order' meaning neat and tidy – as your folded linens ought to be!

Armed to the teeth

If you're an invader and you're armed to the teeth, you might be carrying so many weapons that you literally have one clenched between your teeth. This is one possible explanation of the origin of this phrase, which, it is suggested, harks back to seventeenth-century Caribbean pirates.

Then again, it might be that you are simply 'armed to the teeth' in the metaphorical sense of 'to the teeth', that is fully or completely. For centuries 'to the teeth' has been the equivalent of saying 'up to here' as you indicate your neck.

As cool as a cucumber

The humble cucumber was already being grown in England in the sixteenth century and has always been associated with coolness. whether you're eating it in summer sandwiches. putting it on swollen eyes or adding it to your jug of Pimm's! The original version of the simile. 'as cold as a cucumber'. was apparently applied particularly to women. In 1732. the playwright John Gay referred to 'as cool as a cucumber' as 'a new simile' and it eventually took over from the original expression. It is used to describe someone who is composed and self-possessed.

As sure as eggs is eggs

This expression suggests that something is a certainty or definitely true. The grammatical error gives a clue to its origin as in fact it's nothing to do with eggs. As is often the case with popular expressions. it's a phrase that has become corrupted or misheard over time. and derives from the mathematical certainty that something is 'as sure as x is x'.

As the crow flies

If you refer to the distance between two places 'as the crow flies'. you're talking about the shortest distance between those two points. rather than the distance you would have to travel using paths or roads. The saying derives from the long-held belief that a crow would fly in a straight line back to its nest. although strictly speaking it's the rook rather than the carrion crow that does this.

At a loose end

A nautical expression originally. when you're 'at a loose end' in the figurative sense you have nothing to occupy you. In its literal sense it referred to a rope that was unattached and therefore had been neglected or wasn't serving any purpose.

From the same context comes 'tying up loose ends' – it could be dangerous for ropes on board ship to be left with loose ends. and so the figurative meaning passed into everyday speech. meaning settling the final details of something in order to finish it off.

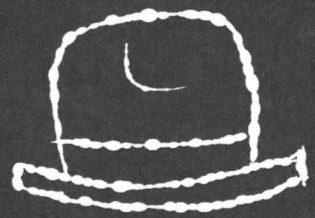

At the drop of a hat

Meaning 'without delay' or 'immediately'. this saying seems to have come from the practice of holding a hat aloft and then dropping it (or lowering it) suddenly as a signal for a race or fight to begin.

At the end of your tether

If you're at the end of your tether, you're exasperated and frustrated. The expression comes from animals being tied with a rope or 'tether' to stop them wandering off. They could graze as far as their tether allowed them to move, but once they reached the end of their tether they could go no further – no doubt feeling very frustrated by this if there was better grazing within sight.

Back of beyond

Now used in a general sense to mean anywhere remote, 'back of beyond' originally comes from nineteenth-century Australia, and is a reference to the vast wilderness lands of that country known as the Outback.

Back to square one

Anyone who has played Snakes and Ladders knows that nothing can be taken for granted as far as progress is concerned. Just as you think you are about to win, you land on that longest of snakes and find yourself, quite literally, back at square one. So the expression has come to be used to suggest any undertaking that has begun, but then for some reason has to be started again from scratch.

It's similar in meaning to 'back to the drawing board'. This refers to boards used by designers and suggests a project that has to go right back to its design or planning stage and be considered again.

Backroom boys

These are the people in an organisation who do the work 'behind the scenes' – they remain anonymous. while other people may take on the public face of the company. The phrase was coined by Lord Beaverbrook in 1941. when he paid tribute to the scientists and technicians who were the 'unsung heroes' of the war effort. saying 'To whom must praise be given? It is the boys in the back rooms.' Of course in these times of political correctness. presumably 'backroom people' would be considered the proper term!

Baker's dozen

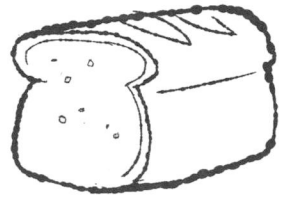

A baker's dozen is thirteen. and the expression is sometimes used in the sense of 'just a little bit extra'. It's commonly thought that it dates from the times when bakers could be fined for selling bread that was under weight. so an extra loaf (or when selling just one loaf. a small extra piece of bread) was added. just to be certain that the correct weight had been reached.

However it's also possible that bakers selling bread on to street vendors to sell added the extra loaf as additional 'commission' to these sellers.

Bald as a coot

What is a 'coot'? And is it really bald? It's a small water bird. and no. it isn't! But it's mainly black with a white stripe at the front of its head. so this might look like a bald spot. In its figurative sense this saying doesn't just refer to a bald patch. though. but suggests that someone is completely bald.

Bandy words

You might talk of 'bandying words' or of a word or a story being 'bandied about'. The word 'bandy' comes from the French bander. meaning to exchange or to toss to and fro. and was used most often in relation to hitting a ball back and forth in an early form of tennis But before the word took on the figurative use we are familiar with today. it then gave rise to the game of bandy. a precursor to hockey. which was popular in Ireland. In this game too. the ball was 'bandied about'.

Today. to bandy words means to argue or answer back. and if something is 'bandied about' it is being spoken of quite casually. or discussed informally.

Incidentally. the shape of the crooked sticks used in the original game of bandy are the source of the expression 'bandy-legged'. meaning bow-legged.

Baptism of fire

Although there is a potential reference here to Christian baptism and indeed to martyrdom by fire, the expression as we know it today – meaning a first painful experience of something – refers to a soldier's first experience of battle, or being 'under fire'.

Barking up the wrong tree

If you're wasting energy on something to no avail, concentrating on the wrong aspect of something, or accusing the wrong person of some misdemeanour, you might be told that you are barking up the wrong tree. The expression comes from the North American practice of using dogs to hunt racoons. This was done after dark, and dogs were used to follow the scent of the unfortunate racoon and bark at the foot of the tree into which it had escaped. Understandably in these conditions, the dogs would sometimes make a mistake and quite literally bark up the wrong tree, no doubt to the relief of the lucky racoon, who would 'live to fight another day'.

Batten down the hatches

Originally used when preparing for bad weather, and still often used in this context today, this term can also be used in the more general sense of 'prepare for trouble'. Ships' hatchways (or hatches) were openings in the deck that allowed you to go below deck, and were usually covered with some kind of grating. When bad weather was expected, the hatches were covered with tarpaulins to stop too much rain getting through. To secure the tarpaulins, wooden strips, or battens, were nailed down round the edges.

The expression had a musical airing as recently as 2012, in the Bob Dylan lyric 'They battened down the hatches but the hatches wouldn't hold', from the song Tempest, describing the sinking of the Titanic.

Battle-axe

No matter how forceful or grumpy an older woman may be, to refer to her as a 'battle-axe' seems a little extreme! So where does the term come from? One theory is that it refers to a formidable nineteenth-century American campaigner for temperance by the name of Carrie Nation, who not only published a magazine called The Hatchet, but campaigned so vigorously that she would smash up taverns with a hatchet, for which over the course of several years she was arrested more than thirty times.

BEAT ABOUT the BUSH

Usually used in the negative 'stop beating about the bush', this very common phrase means to be hesitant or avoid getting to the point. The expression comes from the hunting of game-birds – a beater will flush the birds out by creeping close to them and literally 'beating the bush' so that the hunter can shoot the birds as they fly from cover. This sense of approaching with caution has led to the figurative use.

Beaver away

It's hard to think of an animal that works more diligently than the beaver, shaping wood and building complex dams. So it's no surprise that its name has come to be used in this phrase meaning to work industriously. The related expression 'eager beaver' has a slightly less flattering implication, meaning someone who tries a bit too hard in their keenness to succeed.

Bee in your bonnet

If you had an actual bee in your bonnet, it's safe to say you'd be rather distracted and this would be the only thing you could think about at that moment. From this comes the figurative use of the phrase to suggest an obsession or preoccupation with one thing or idea.

Below the belt

An unfair or unscrupulous tactic or remark could be described as being 'below the belt'. It's something that's simply not sporting, or to use another very English phrase, 'not cricket'. It arises, in fact, from another sport – boxing. Rules for the sport were first drafted in 1743 by the boxer Jack Broughton, although it is the Marquess of Queensberry's rules, introduced in 1867, that form the basis of the regulations for modern boxing. One of the new rules introduced when the sport was first regulated specified that any blow to the body below the line of the waist, or belt, was prohibited.

Best laid plans

Often used just in the short form 'The best laid plans...' with the rest of the saying being implied rather than spoken, this is an observation that you can plan all you like but events can overtake you or disrupt your intentions. The full saying is 'The best laid plans of mice and men go oft astray', and it's a quotation from the Robert Burns poem To a Mouse, although the original uses Scottish dialect and Burns wrote 'schemes' rather than plans. But like many mis-quotations, the incorrect form is now the one used most often. This line of the poem also inspired the title of the 1937 John Steinbeck novel Of Mice and Men.

Best thing since sliced bread

This is a relatively recent expression, as you'd expect, given that it refers to the automated process of producing a loaf that was pre-sliced rather than having to be cut at home. This innovation appeared in the first half of the twentieth century and, for reasons that are now unclear, members of the US armed forces seem to have considered it such an achievement that they coined this phrase as an indication of their approval of something.

Between the devil and the deep blue sea

If you're in an impossible predicament, where neither of your options is desirable, you're 'between the devil and the deep blue sea'. The devil in this instance isn't the horned representation of evil, but rather a seam in a ship's hull – so being trapped between that and the sea was not a good place to be. A more modern equivalent might be 'between a rock and a hard place', an American phrase that has become common in the English-speaking world. Of course if you have to choose between two equally unappealing outcomes, you may find that you have been forced 'out of the frying pan into the fire'!

Between you, me and the gatepost

Meaning 'strictly between ourselves', this expression started out as 'between you, me and the bedpost'. This was alluding to a four-poster bed and suggested two people tucked away behind the curtains of such a bed having a private conversation. But given that any sort of post was a lifeless, 'deaf' object, the gatepost is equally good at conveying the meaning, and may have been a variant coined by people too poor to have a great deal of experience of four-poster beds!

Big cheese

A 'big cheese' is someone really important, but however much you enjoy dairy products you might be forgiven for thinking that it's not the most flattering comparison you could make. In fact, you'd be right to be cautious, as the word didn't originate as 'cheese' at all, but as the Persian chiz, meaning 'thing'. In Victorian England, the expression 'the real thing' was in common use and in time this mutated into 'the real chiz'. Predictably enough, after being misheard, the saying became 'the real cheese' and then, on crossing the Atlantic, it mutated once again to become 'the big cheese'.

Blow hot and cold

If you're inconsistent in your reaction or relationship to something or someone, you might be accused of 'blowing hot and cold'. The saying comes directly from the Aesop fable The Satyr and the Traveller. The satyr meets a traveller in the woods and sees him blowing on his hands to warm them. He then invites the man to his home and gives him hot soup, which the traveller blows on to cool it. The satyr is having none of it, and sends the man away, saying he doesn't want anything to do with someone who can blow hot and cold with the same breath. It might seem like a bit of an over-reaction, but looking at it from the allegorical point of view, you can see why it could be a good idea to steer clear of someone who blows hot and cold.

Bob's your uncle

Meaning 'there you have it' or 'everything is sorted', this catchy little phrase is often added on to explanations of how to do something. Its origins are somewhat obscure. One theory is that it was coined after the nineteenth-century politician A.J. Balfour rose rather swiftly though the ranks thanks to the intervention of his uncle, Lord (Robert) Salisbury. Another theory references a musical revue of the 1920s, entitled simply Bob's Your Uncle, which may have captured the public imagination – though exactly why the phrase then came to be used as it is may never be known for certain.

Sometimes the expression is extended to 'Bob's your uncle and Fanny's your aunt' – although in some places the aunt is Nellie – and sometimes it is used in the mock-formal version 'Robert is your mother's brother'. Regardless of its origin, it's a phrase that has been widely used for at least a century and seems to be as popular as ever.

Bottom line

Now a very common phrase meaning the most important fact to be considered, or the end result or conclusion of something, 'the bottom line' refers in its literal sense to the last line on a row of accounts. This shows the total, which is the final, and arguably the most important, figure.

Box and cox

Boxing and coxing implies doing two things alternately or sharing responsibilities. More generally, however, it has evolved to mean having to shuffle things around or deal with several options or situations at once. It comes from a nineteenth-century play, Box and Cox, about two men who rent the same room from an unscrupulous landlady – as one of them works by day and the other by night, neither of them is aware that they are in fact sharing the same room.

Break the ice

From the practice of literally breaking up frozen waters to allow ships and boats to pass, comes this expression, which originally meant forging a path for others to follow. Now it's taken on the broader meaning of breaking down social formalities so that everyone is relaxed and can get on with a business or social activity.

Other icy expressions include 'that cuts no ice with me', meaning 'that makes little impression' or 'that doesn't change my mind', although the use of ice here is obscure. You might also be 'skating on thin ice', which carries a more obvious meaning – you're taking a risk and you know there's a chance that you might 'come a cropper'!

BRING TO HEEL

Just as you would train a dog to come to heel, you can figuratively 'bring someone to heel' by bringing them under control.

Bunny boiler

This is a good example of a phrase that is commonly used and understood, with an origin that can be traced without any doubt or debate whatsoever. Meaning a vindictive, and possibly somewhat unhinged, woman who is obsessed with or stalks an ex, the phrase comes from the grisly scene in the 1987 film Fatal Attraction where Alex, played by Glenn Close, kills and cooks her ex-lover's daughter's pet rabbit. Although the phrase 'bunny boiler' isn't actually used in the movie, the concept must have appealed as a metaphor of the 'woman scorned' and pretty soon someone came up with this witty alliterative phrase that's now in everyday use.

Burn the candle at both ends

It would be hard to do this today, with modern candles having a wick visible only at the top. But in times gone by, tallow candles (made from animal fat) often had a wick that protruded at both ends. The candle could be held in a bracket, thus allowing both ends to be lit at the same time. However, it was considered very extravagant to do this and 'burning the candle at both ends' was frowned upon. Over the years, of course, the literal meaning has become obscured, and the phrase has come to refer to getting up early as well as staying up late, with the implication that someone who does this is tiring himself or herself out. whether through working hard or playing hard.

Staying up late is also referenced in the expression 'burn the midnight oil'. In this instance the implication is that you are studying or working late – by the light of an oil lamp – rather than partying. The term seems to have been coined by seventeenth-century writer Francis Quarles. who wrote of 'our midday sweat. our midnight oil'. but it harks back to an earlier expression. In the sixteenth century something was said to 'smell of the oil' (again from an oil lamp) when it was clear that a lot of work had gone into it.

Burn your boats

By burning your boats (or indeed burning your bridges) you are committing yourself to a course of action from which there is no turning back. In today's military parlance. you'd say you had no 'exit strategy'. Although the expression seems only to have been used since the nineteenth century, it has its origin in the tactics of ancient warfare. when armies were expected to have such commitment to a cause that they would not leave open any kind of escape route. They would burn the boats in which they arrived to fight their enemies and so be expected to defeat them or die in the attempt.

Bury the hatchet

Native Americans would, in times gone by, quite literally bury their hatchets and other weapons of war when hostilities were ended and they sat with their former enemies to smoke a peace pipe. It was seen as a sign of commitment to the ending of a war. These days, if you bury the hatchet you're putting a dispute behind you or agreeing to 'let bygones be bygones'.

Busman's holiday

A 'busman's holiday' is when you spend your leisure time doing the same thing that you normally do for a living. It's believed to have originated in the days of horse-drawn coaches or omnibuses, when presumably if a bus driver wanted a break, he had no option but to travel this way. Some have gone so far as to suggest that these drivers were so committed to their horses that they travelled on the buses on their days off to keep an eye on them.

Butter wouldn't melt

In its full form – 'butter wouldn't melt in his/her mouth' – this saying originally implied that the person in question was so cool (in the sense of aloof or unfriendly) that their mouth wouldn't even be warm enough to melt butter. But these days it's more often used humorously, and frequently in the short form, to suggest that someone who is trying to look innocent is anything but!

By and large

Coming from a nautical source, and meaning 'in general', the term referred to a helmsman's ability to keep control of his ship when sailing 'by and large', which meant steering slightly off the line of the wind and thus not needing to make constant adjustments. So it gained the sense of not needing to be as precise or to be as alert and from this took on its present meaning.

By hook or by crook

Meaning 'by any means', or 'one way or another', this expression dates from medieval times, when its meaning was predictably more literal – and in fact referred to a quite specific way of doing something. Its use originated from the right of tenants on an estate to gather as much wood as they could reach using only a billhook and a shepherd's crook. This, of course, limited the amount they could gather, but the expression may have come to imply that some degree of ingenuity or cunning was required to make the most of the opportunity.

Call a spade a spade

If you speak plainly or bluntly, you are, today, 'calling a spade a spade'. However, in ancient Greece, you would have called a fig a fig and a tub a tub. Somewhere around the sixteenth century the word 'spade' became a substitute for 'tub' and has stuck ever since.

Carry coals to Newcastle

If you are carrying coals (or taking coals) to Newcastle you're doing something unnecessary, because you are taking something to an area where it is already plentiful. This expression exists in various forms in many other cultures, with the French, for example, referring to 'carrying water to the river' and the Greeks talking of 'carrying owls to Athens'!

Carte blanche

This term has a military origin and comes from the French, its literal meaning being 'blank paper'. It was used at times of unconditional surrender – the defeated force would issue a blank paper on which the victors could write their own terms and conditions (or as they are more often known today T&Cs), knowing that they would be accepted. Now the term is widely used in its figurative sense, meaning having free rein or total freedom to do something the way you choose.

Cat nap

A short refreshing sleep has long been known as a cat nap – but quite why the phrase should be used for something so brief when cats are quite capable of sleeping all day isn't clear. Maybe the suggestion is that they can wake up and be alert very quickly, no matter how long they've been asleep. In modern times, you're more likely to hear the phrase 'power nap' – and the benefits of this short sleep (at your desk if needs be) are extolled by many prominent business people and politicians.

Catch red-handed

If you catch someone red-handed you catch them in the act of committing a crime, figuratively if not literally before they have had time to wash the blood off their hands. Two similar legal terms preceded this expression – 'redhand' and 'with red hand – but it is Walter Scott who is attributed with first using the expression in the form we use today.

Catch 22

A catch 22 situation is a paradox or deadlock in which you can't win. It's a good example of a phrase coined in literature which then enters the language because it sums something up succinctly. Not that there aren't other phrases that do the same job – you might also say that you're 'damned if you do and damned if you don't' or you might talk of 'heads I win, tails you lose'.

Catch-22 was the title of a book by Joseph Heller, first published in 1961. It describes the activities of airmen in the Second World War and the 'catch' of the title was this – an airman could be excused from a mission on grounds of insanity. But if he claimed that he was insane as an excuse not to fly, he was declared to be of rational mind (because he sensibly wanted to avoid being killed) and therefore sent on the mission.

Chalk and cheese

Used to suggest that two things are 'poles apart' and not alike in any way, the saying 'as different as chalk and cheese' derives simply from the fact that chalk and cheese (or some types of cheese at least) look very similar on the surface, but couldn't be more different in reality.

Less common nowadays are the variants 'he doesn't know chalk from cheese' or 'he couldn't tell chalk from cheese', mild insults implying that someone can't differentiate between two things when the difference should be obvious.

Cherry picking

Anyone who has participated in this activity in its most literal sense knows that it is a practice that is undertaken by hand – and as such it gives the picker the opportunity to select only the best fruit. In the business world, 'cherry picking' has come to have a similar connotation – in a takeover situation, the new business owner can select the best-performing or most profitable sectors of another enterprise, at the expense of those areas with lesser success. It can be used with reference to personnel too – the best people for the job might be chosen while those less talented are sidelined.

CHIP IN

If lots of people 'chip in' to buy something it means that they all make a contribution into a central fund. The term comes from the game of poker in which 'chips', representing money, are placed in the 'pot' or 'kitty' by all the players.

Linked to this is the expression 'when the chips are down', meaning when there's no going back or there is no room for manoeuvre. In poker, it means that the money has been put down on the table, decisions have been made and the game is reaching its peak.

Clapped out

Meaning dilapidated, and more often than not used to describe old cars that are in poor condition, clapped out can also mean 'exhausted' and this is where the original derivation lies. In the days when hare-coursing was common, a hare that was exhausted from running and which stopped to catch its breath would sit up on its haunches panting. As its chest moved in and out its front legs would move, giving the impression that it was sitting up and clapping. So it's from the poor exhausted 'clapped out' hare that we get the expression we use today.

Clean bill of health

It's always good to know that your doctor has given you a 'clean bill of health', meaning that you are 'as fit as a fiddle'. The bill in question was originally not a declaration that concerned just one person, but a certificate (bill) given to the captain of a ship that was sailing from a port where there might have been infectious diseases. A 'clean bill of health' stated that there was no infection in the port or on the ship, and was a vital document for the captain to have in his possession in order to be allowed to dock at the next port.

CLEAR the DECKS

In the days of great sea battles, it was a good idea, for obvious reasons, to clear the ship's decks of anything unnecessary that could be tripped over or that would get in the way of firing the guns. Nowadays, when we talk of clearing the decks we mean much the same – not decks, of course, unless by chance you actually are on a boat at the time, but getting rid of any unnecessary clutter, especially if we're doing it in preparation for something.

Climb on the bandwagon

If you climb on the bandwagon, you are figuratively 'getting on board' with a cause or a current trend, hoping to benefit yourself in some way. Its origin is quite literal – years ago in the USA, bands would parade the streets on wagons to advertise public meetings, often of a political nature. Local dignitaries would show support for a cause or a candidate by climbing onto their particular wagon as it passed through the town.

Of course if you are simply 'on the wagon' this means something else entirely, although this phrase too does have a literal connection to physical wagons. In this case, it was water wagons, which were used to spray water on the dusty streets of nineteenth-century American cities. Those who had 'taken the pledge', that is sworn to avoid alcohol for the rest of their lives, were said to have commented that they would rather drink from the water wagon than partake of alcoholic liquor. From this we get today's phrase 'on the wagon', although it may not always be used in the sense of a lifetime pledge! Similarly, anyone who tries to stop drinking but then lapses is now said to have 'fallen off the wagon'.

Close of play

It's not uncommon for someone, in a working context, to promise that they will achieve something 'by close of play'. They mean by the end of the working day. It's a cricketing term, with 'close of play' being the end of that day's play but not necessarily the end of the match.

Close ranks

When you close ranks you are putting up a united front. On the battlefield, an army would close ranks, that is literally stand shoulder to shoulder, as they approached an enemy. Having no gaps between them, they presented a solid wall of attackers, wielding swords, guns or bayonets.

Coast is clear

Most often used when you're up to no good and you don't want anyone to see you, the expression 'the coast is clear' is a form of reassurance that it's safe to go ahead with whatever it is you have planned. Predictably enough, it's a seafaring term and was used to describe a situation where it was safe to land. More often than not, this was by smugglers who wanted to be certain that the coastguards were not lying in wait!

Come up to scratch

Before the days of starting blocks and marked tracks, runners would line up at the start of a race along a line scratched in the ground. Boxers did something similar, with each contestant having to have one foot against the line before the bout could begin. From this, 'coming up to scratch' came to imply doing things properly or reaching a certain standard.

Cook the books

Instead of 'cooking the books', these days someone might equally be accused of 'creative accounting'. Whatever the preferred phrase, the implication is clear – by cooking the books you are making changes to accounts in order to profit or to avoid paying taxes. The word 'cook' originally meant altering something, or changing it into something else. Thus it came to be used for turning raw ingredients into an edible meal. So cooking the books may not necessarily involve heat, or producing anything tasty, but it does involve changing something to your advantage.

Cry wolf

Another saying that comes from Aesop's fables, 'cry wolf' refers to the story of the shepherd boy who repeatedly shouted 'Wolf!' just for the fun of seeing people run to help. But of course when a real wolf came along, no one took him seriously. The expression is now used to describe any situation where someone asks for help when they don't need it or complains about something when there's nothing really wrong.

Cupboard love

Cupboard love is affection that may not be genuine, but is simply shown out of self-interest or in order to gain something. It suggests the pretence of love that children will show to someone who is going to indulge them with treats from the cupboard – although many a pet owner will testify that animals are equally capable of this approach.

CUT AND DRIED

Before timber can be burnt, it has to be cut down and dried – when it's reached that state it's ready. Equally, anything that is metaphorically 'cut and dried' is ready, arranged in advance or finished.

Cut your coat according to your cloth

This is sage advice to live within your means. As you must create a garment from the amount of cloth you have available. so you should spend only as much as you can afford. Presumably this expression dates from the days before credit cards were widely available. as today this advice can all too easily be ignored.

Dark horse

This term stems from the world of horse racing. but it doesn't have anything to do with the colour of the horse. Rather. it's a horse about which the public has been 'kept in the dark' – in other words no one knows much about it. although it may have promise. If a person is a dark horse. they may equally have hidden talents. or they may have some sort of secret that comes to light to the surprise of others.

Dead as a doornail

A doornail was the knob on which a door knocker would be struck – presumably having been hit repeatedly in this way it was considered 'dead'. More common today. perhaps. is 'dead as a dodo'. Famously extinct. the odd-looking dodo died out in 1681 but lives on in this common expression.

Devil's advocate

If you're playing devil's advocate, you're arguing against someone else on a topic – but not because you necessarily believe in the opposing argument. You're just doing it for the sake of testing the argument or so that the other person can consider another viewpoint. The term is used in a general sense in all sorts of everyday situations, but in its formal usage (and in its original Latin advocatus diaboli), it is actually the role of a Roman Catholic official who is given the job of arguing against the proposed beatification or canonisation of someone who has died. Again, the idea is that this will ensure that the argument is seen from all possible angles.

Do porridge

Slang for 'spend time in prison', the origin of this phrase is said to be from the rhyming slang 'borage and thyme', meaning 'time' – and of course 'doing time' is itself another slang term for being 'behind bars'. It may also be something to do with the fact that porridge was once a staple food in prison, but whatever the origin, anyone in the 1970s who wasn't familiar with the term soon came to understand it due to the popularity of the TV sitcom Porridge.

Dog's life

If you're thinking of a pampered pooch you might well consider that a dog's life is a rather good one. In fact, this saying dates back to the days when dogs were little more than household servants and used for hunting or protection as much as companionship. Thus, 'it's a dog's life' has come to suggest a miserable existence, although the more we spoil our pets the more the phrase is used ironically.

There are many more phrases that mention dogs. There are 'dog-eared' pages that are crumpled at the corner, resembling the turned-down ears of dogs, for example, or there is the clergyman's 'dog collar', which again is self-explanatory.

Other figurative uses of the dog include 'dog in the manger', a reference to the dog in a fable who occupied a manger in order to stop other animals from eating the hay, even though he didn't want it himself. So the expression came to be used to describe someone who acts out of spite.

'Dog days' are the hot days of July and August which coincide with the appearance of the Dog Star (Sirius) in the same part of the sky as the sun. The Romans believed that the star must contribute to the heat.

Last, but by no means least, remember that 'every dog has its day'. This means that we all have our moment of success. It's not recorded why dogs are named in this particular expression, but it's reassuring all the same.

Don't look a gift horse in the mouth

The age of a horse can be judged by looking at its teeth, so looking in its mouth would give you a fair idea of its age, its health and thus its worth. But it would be rude to look too closely at the value of something given as a gift, so this expression suggests that you should simply accept gracefully.

Doolally

All kinds of things might send you doolally, or a little bit crazy, but in nineteenth-century India, soldiers were sent to Deo-lali, a town near Bombay, while they awaited their passage home. There wasn't much to do, it was hot, and ships were often delayed, so this combination may have made some of them start to go a little bit nutty.

Down in the dumps

It's not much fun being down in the dumps. You feel low and depressed and there's not much to smile about. But why 'the dumps'? It's nothing to do with the English word 'dump' as we use it now, but is probably a corruption of a word from other languages – the Swedish dumpin (melancholy), the Dutch dompig (damp) and/or the German dumpf (gloomy, damp).

Dry run

Practice bombing flights were undertaken by the RAF in the Second World War. They went through all the procedures of the planned attack, but without actually dropping the bombs. These practice missions became known as 'dry runs' and the term soon passed into general use to describe a rehearsal or practice before an event.

Dutch courage

In the seventeenth and eighteenth centuries, Britain and Holland had all sorts of disputes, from trade disagreements to all-out wars. From this, many expressions arose that included the word 'Dutch', and most were none too flattering. 'Dutch courage' is a stiff drink to bolster you before some kind of daunting task and was a term coined by British sailors who believed that their counterparts drank gin before battles!

You might also have a 'Dutch uncle' who is someone very critical, or you might go on a 'Dutch treat', which is not a treat at all as you pay your own way. Nowadays this last term isn't necessarily used in such a negative way, but is simply used in the form 'going Dutch' meaning to share the cost.

Dyed in the wool

Englands wool and cloth trade was at one time a huge industry, and as in any manufacturing process, there were various ways of preparing goods for sale or export. Coloured cloth was either 'dyed in the wool' – that is the wool was dyed before being woven into cloth – or dyed after weaving. Cloth that was dyed in the wool tended to retain its colour for longer and this implied durability and reliability has been retained in the figurative use of the phrase to mean thorough, genuine or out-and-out.

Ear to the ground

If you're keeping your ear to the ground, you're trying to keep abreast of what is happening or to find something out as soon as possible. The analogy is said to be with trackers, Native Americans in particular, who would quite literally put their ear to the ground in order to listen to distant movement and anticipate the arrival of herds of prey or indeed enemies.

EAT HUMBLE PIE

If you've been forced to admit that you're wrong, or if you have to climb down from a position of superiority, you may have to eat humble pie. This doesn't involve literally eating anything, of course, but the original expression – 'eat umble pie' – did. 'Umbles' is an archaic word for offal, and in the days when great hunts took place, the lord of the manor and his guests would dine on the finest venison, while the huntsmen and those of lower social standing would dine on a pie made from the umbles. So in its literal usage, eating umble pie did suggest that you were somehow inferior, and the obvious pun on the word gave rise to the expression we know today.

Eavesdropping

If you're secretly listening in to a conversation that you shouldn't be, you are eavesdropping. The word originated in the days when all houses were obliged to have space around them to allow water to run off the eaves – this was known as the eaves-drop. So someone who stood in this space – close enough to the walls to be able to hear what was going on inside the house – was an eavesdropper. This wouldn't happen in modern times – what with terraced houses, guttering and insulated walls, an eavesdropper has to find more imaginative ways to listen in on others' conversations.

Egg on

If you're encouraging someone or inciting them to do something, you could be said to be 'egging them on'. The saying has nothing to do with eggs as we use the word today, but comes from a Scandinavian word meaning 'edge', so when you're egging someone on you're actually edging them, or urging them, forward.

Elephant in the room

The 'elephant in the room' is the really obvious topic or subject that everyone is deliberately ignoring. The imagery is of something so huge you couldn't miss it, but people are too embarrassed to mention it. Sadly, no one seems to know where the phrase originated, but it seems to have been used from the 1950s onwards.

Elvis has left the building

One of the first megastars in the world of music, Elvis Presley had a huge and dedicated fan base. It's alleged that this saying was coined by the manager of a venue in which he performed, who had to find a way of convincing the screaming fans that their hero was not going to do any more encores and that they should go home! It's now used to imply that something is over and done with or complete, but it's often said too in a humorous manner in all sorts of situations with the appropriate name replacing Elvis's.

Face the music

By facing the music you are accepting the consequences of your actions. The origin of this saying is uncertain, but there are two plausible theories. One is that it derives from the stage, where actors faced the orchestra pit when they were 'treading the boards', in which case facing the music certainly might make you nervous, and there is the added implication that as the actor steps onto the stage there is no going back.

The other explanation may lie in the ceremony of a disgraced soldier being 'drummed out' of the army – charges would be read out while drums were beaten and the soldier was formally dismissed. Less musical, of course, but no doubt a daunting experience and this explanation may fit better with the modern meaning of having to face up to the consequences of some misdemeanour or other.

Fair to middling

Meaning slightly above average. this expression seems to have come from systems of grading produce or manufactured goods. Various scales were used as grades in different fields of manufacturing or agriculture. but the principle was the same. In cotton production for example. the grades of cotton ranged from 'inferior' to 'fine'. Sitting somewhere around the middle of such a scale. fabric that was 'fair to middling' was better than some. but not the best.

Fall between two stools

If you fall between two stools you are undecided. or it's uncertain which course of action is best. It's not certain why stools in particular should be used in this phrase – in France they say 'sit between two chairs'. Of course if you are deliberately keeping your options open you may decide that you are better off 'sitting on the fence!'

Fall guy

A loser or a victim of deception. The term comes from fixed wrestling matches. where one wrestler would agree to 'take a fall' so that the other could win. Part of the agreement was that the 'fall guy' wouldn't be treated too harshly by his opponent. but in reality the winner often failed to stick to this part of the bargain. giving this term the sense that the fall guy has been somehow tricked or duped.

Famous last words

Many great people down the centuries have left us with wise and memorable 'last words' from their deathbeds, although we'll never know for sure whether they are all genuine. However, the use of the phrase 'famous last words' has come to be a mildly sarcastic, or even self-mocking, observation that something probably won't work out quite as well as planned. It was popularised by RAF bomber crews in the Second World War as a response to official statements that minimised the risks they faced in forthcoming missions.

Feather in your cap

In many Asian and Native American cultures it was customary to add a feather to your headgear as a symbol of having killed an enemy. In sporting circles this has sometimes been done too – the hunter who killed the first woodcock traditionally wore a feather in his cap. In a figurative sense, the saying has come to be used to symbolise a personal achievement, or something that earns you praise – without necessarily killing anything or anybody!

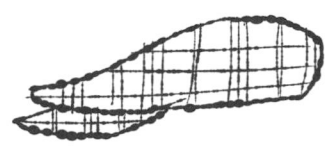

Field day

If you have a 'field day', the implication is that you are enjoying freedom, unconditional fun or an exciting opportunity. Strange, then, that the term comes from the military practice of field manoeuvres, which presumably were much more closely regulated occasions, although it's probable that they involved a fair bit of noise and running around, which may have led to the present-day meaning.

Fish out of water

It doesn't take much imagination to realise that a fish out of water would be very uncomfortable indeed, so someone who is 'out of their comfort zone' could also be described as a fish out of water. It's actually a very old phrase and in the Prologue to the Canterbury Tales, Chaucer refers to a 'cloisterless monk' being 'like to a fish that is waterless'.

Flash in the pan

This is something like a 'nine-day wonder' – something that fails, dies down or becomes unpopular after a very promising start. 'Flash in the pan' derives from the use of flintlock guns, where the powder would flash in the priming pan, but the charge didn't always go off: in other words the flash was 'something and nothing'. A nine-day wonder is thought to refer to dogs – as puppies are blind for the first week or so, so people may initially be 'blind' to the reality of a situation, but they soon see it for what it is.

Flavour of the month

In its literal sense, this was a popular advertising gimmick. It is thought to have originated in ice-cream parlours, who promoted their business with varying flavours of the month, often offered at a reduced price to attract customers. Now, of course, it simply describes anyone or anything that is popular or fashionable for a short space of time.

Freelance

Anyone who works 'freelance' today does so as an independent self-employed worker. The term was coined by Sir Walter Scott in his medieval romance Ivanhoe, published in 1820. The 'freelance' in this context was a medieval warrior who was free to offer his services to whoever was prepared to pay him, rather than having feudal loyalty to a particular lord – in other words a medieval mercenary.

Freeze the balls off a brass monkey

As winter sets in there will always be days when someone tells you that it's cold enough to 'freeze the balls off a brass monkey'. However, this expression has nothing to do with anatomy. A 'brass monkey' was a metal plate fixed to the deck of a ship, on which cannon balls were stacked. When it was very cold, the brass would contract and the carefully piled cannon balls would roll off.

Fresh as a daisy

It's nice to feel 'fresh as a daisy' – not at all tired and 'bright as a button'. The expression derives from the old belief that the daisy doesn't get tired because it 'sleeps' at night, closing at sunset and opening in the morning. Of course it's not the only flower that does this, but as it's a common flower and would have been known to most people, perhaps that's the reason why it came to be the flower used in this phrase.

From pillar to post

The ancient game of 'real tennis', still played today by some, is the origin of this expression. The court contains a number of protrusions – the pillars and posts of the saying – which can make the ball fly off in unexpected directions, so the term has come to mean moving from one thing to another without any clear objective or direction.

Full monty

Meaning 'everything' or 'the whole lot', the origin of the phrase 'the full monty' is obscure, although there are several theories. The most plausible seems to be the suggestion that it refers to suits bought from Burton's the tailor – a company founded by Sir Montague Burton, or 'Monty'. A complete three-piece suit bought from one of his shops was colloquially referred to by the staff as 'the full monty'. Of course since the film of the same name in the 1990s, the expression may more readily bring to mind images of undressing rather than dressing up!

Get down to brass tacks

In old-fashioned drapers' shops, brass tacks would be driven into the counter at evenly spaced distances to serve as handy guides for measuring lengths of cloth. From this comes the expression 'getting down to brass tacks', meaning determining exactly what is required, or in other words, getting down to the 'nitty-gritty'.

Get hitched

Getting hitched means getting married, with 'hitch' being used in this context as the equivalent of 'tying the knot' – a hitch being the nautical term used for several types of knot used to fasten one thing temporarily to another. When it comes to getting married, however, the 'joining together' is intended to be a more permanent arrangement!

Get out of bed the wrong side

If you're in a bad mood in the morning, you may be accused of getting out of bed the wrong side. In practical terms, of course, there's usually only one side you would get out of, but the saying is probably loosely connected to the superstition that it was unlucky to put your left foot on the ground first when getting out of bed. Those of a superstitious nature will also avoid putting on the left shoe first. These superstitions are also linked to the expression we now use for making a bad initial impression: 'getting off on the wrong foot'.

Get the sack

Used since the nineteenth century, when itinerant tradesmen carried the tools of their trade in a sack, this expression has come to mean being dismissed from a job. When a job was finished, or the workman was dismissed for some reason, he quite literally 'got the sack', took his belongings and tools with him, and set off in search of employment.

Get your goat

As an expression meaning to make you angry or annoyed. this is a rather gentle phrase. avoiding the use of excessive expletives. No one is quite sure where it comes from. although there is one possibility that has been put forward. It's said that in years gone by. racehorse owners would calm a nervous horse before a race by putting a goat in its stall. To unsettle the horse again. it would only take someone to sneak in and 'get your goat'. leaving the horse once again jittery and unlikely to run well. It may be a far-fetched explanation. but until something better comes to light. it certainly conjures up an amusing image.

Get your second wind

When running a long race. athletes will initially get out of breath. but as the event continues. their breathing will settle into a rhythm that gives them the energy to continue. known as the 'second wind'. This has now come to be used to signify a situation in which someone overcomes tiredness or exhaustion. whether literally or metaphorically. and has the energy to carry on.

Gloves are off

When the gloves are off. there is a suggestion that. figuratively speaking. a battle of some sort is about to commence and that it's going to be a tough one. with little mercy shown. The saying comes from boxing. where after centuries of bare-fist matches. gloves were introduced by the Queensberry Rules in the nineteenth century. So an allusion to the gloves being off suggests going back to a more basic and brutal kind of fight.

Go ballistic

If someone goes ballistic they 'fly off the handle' and explode in a rage. The analogy is to a modern ballistic missile which is set on its course and then left unguided to fall freely towards its target.

Go berserk

Going berserk suggests some kind of frenzy, going a bit crazy. A berserker was a Norse warrior who fought with outstanding courage and great ferocity, reputedly without armour. The name came from 'bear sark' which meant bear coat and the berserkers even believed that they took on the spirit or shape of a bear whilst fighting. It's fascinating to think that a term which dates back to the first millennium is now commonly used and widely understood in the twenty-first century.

Go for gold

Although gold medals had been awarded to winning competitors for at least a hundred years, it wasn't until the 1980 Winter Olympics that the phrase 'go for gold' was first heard. It was the American team who were first urged to win by 'going for gold' and the expression soon caught on with other teams. Now it's also acquired the figurative sense of 'aim for success'.

GOOD RUN FOR YOUR MONEY

If you got a good run for your money at the races, it meant that the horse
you'd backed provided you with good entertainment and an exciting race, even
if it didn't win. Now the term is used more broadly to apply to any competitive
situation – someone who gives you a 'good run for your money' will prove a
tough or well-matched competitor, even if at the outcome you are the one
expected to win.

Grasp the nettle

If you have to face some sort of unpleasant situation or undertake a task that you'd rather not. it's best to tackle it boldly. head on: that way it won't be as bad. The allusion is to stinging nettles. which can leave you in pain if touched tentatively. but which are much less likely to sting if you grasp them firmly.

Hair of the dog (that bit you)

It was believed in times gone by that a dog bite could be cured by applying hair from the dog that attacked you to the wound. Quite why this was meant to help is unclear. but as with many folk remedies it was a firmly held belief. In fact it was so widely accepted that the remedy has given rise to a common modern phrase that is used to describe a potential hangover cure: drinking more alcohol. Although there are all sorts of weird and wonderful hangover 'cures'. there's some basis in fact for this particular one – if you're suffering from a withdrawal from alcohol poisoning. a little alcohol could temporarily make you feel better. But in the long term. it's probably better to stick with the tried and tested formula: plenty of liquids and some light food.

Hammer and tongs

Someone undertaking a task and going at it 'hammer and tongs' is doing it with great force or even violence. This saying dates from the days when blacksmiths were far more common than they are today, and in order to do essential work in shaping hot iron, the smith would hold it with tongs and shape it with a hammer on an anvil. Of course he had to work quickly, to 'strike while the iron is hot', in order to get the best result.

Hand over fist

These days, 'hand over fist' is usually used in the context of the easy and plentiful making of money, similar in meaning to 'coining it in' or 'raking it in'. The analogy is to the nautical hauling in of a rope which has to be done smoothly and quickly and the phrase came to be used for any activity that required something to be grabbed by hand unhesitatingly.

Handle with kid gloves

Kid gloves, made from the skin of young goats, were especially delicate and were also a somewhat expensive accessory. Initially, to nineteenth-century fashion experts, they were considered somewhat ostentatious, but in time it seems their fashion value became appreciated and they even gave rise to this saying, meaning to handle a situation or person delicately or carefully.

Happy as a clam

Just how you choose to express your happiness seems to depend on what part of the world you live in. This saying is most common in the USA. but it probably doesn't. as many people think. refer to the 'smiley' appearance of a partially opened clam. Instead. it was actually. in its full form. 'as happy as a clam at high water'. in other words safe from predators. although admittedly it's still rather a stretch of the imagination to think of a humble clam as being particularly cheery under these circumstances.

In the UK. you're more likely to be 'as happy as a sandboy'. These were young men who delivered sand to homes and places of work in the eighteenth and nineteenth centuries. It was used as a basic floor covering. and some of the sandboys' best customers would have been pubs. where sand was the precursor to sawdust (as in 'spit and sawdust' bars). The sandboys may have been happy because they could collect sand free from the beach and then sell it. or perhaps it had more to do with taking refreshments in those drinking establishments!

Around the other side of the world. in Australia and New Zealand. the expression 'as happy as Larry' is the phrase most commonly used. There's debate about who Larry was. It may be a reference to the nineteenth-century Australian boxer Larry Foley. who never lost a fight and was said to have earned as much as £1000 for winning a bout – that's a lot of money in the 1870s. so whether or not he was the source of the phrase. we can probably assume without any doubt that he was happy!

HAT TRICK

This term is used regularly, particularly in sporting contexts, to describe achieving three successes in a row, for example a footballer scoring three goals in the same match. But what does that have to do with hats? Or indeed tricks? There are various theories. It's generally agreed that the term originated on the cricket pitch, where in order to achieve the original hat trick, a bowler had to dismiss three batsmen with three consecutive deliveries. At that point either his team-mates held a whip-round and bought him a new hat, or a hat was passed round to collect money for the lucky bowler. Either is equally plausible.

The term 'hat trick' may have come from this, and in addition been a reference to something magical – as in a magician's hat trick – where something surprising is pulled out of nowhere. It's easy to see how this association could be made.

Unrelated to the concept of three successes, the phrase was also used in the House of Commons in the nineteenth century, when an MP who reserved his seat by leaving his top hat on it was said to have 'done a hat trick'.

Head over heels

When you stop to think about it, there would be no reason to use this phrase literally – our head is always over our heels. In fact, the expression, which originated in the fourteenth century, began life as 'heels over head', and referred to a cartwheel or somersault. At some point the phrase became 'head over heels', although oddly it still meant the same thing. It then came to be used figuratively, presumably expressing the idea that someone was so happy they were turning cartwheels, and in its modern usage it's most often found in the phrase 'head over heels in love'.

Hide your light under a bushel

If you are modest about your abilities, or don't want to brag about your talents, you might be said to be hiding your light under a bushel. The implication is clear, but what exactly was a 'bushel'? It was actually a measure (equivalent to eight gallons) used for goods such as grain. But in time the wooden or earthenware containers themselves, which were used to measure out this quantity, came to be known as bushels, and it's under one of these that you could – if you really wanted to – hide a light.

Hit the hay

This comes from the same source as 'hit the sack', both of which mean to go to bed. The expression comes from the days when many people didn't have the luxury of a proper bed – or certainly not of a proper mattress – so they slept on sacks filled with hay or straw.

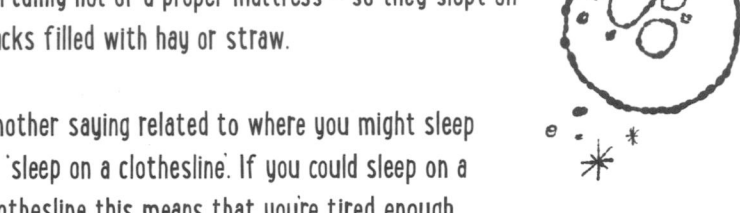

Another saying related to where you might sleep is 'sleep on a clothesline'. If you could sleep on a clothesline this means that you're tired enough to sleep anywhere, and this expression dates from more recent times. In the depression of the 1930s, homeless men could sleep cheaply in establishments where they sat in rows on benches with a rope strung in front of them. Draped over the rope, they would get a better sleep than if they were on the floor – until the morning came and someone appeared with a knife and went round cutting the ropes! Incidentally, this is unconnected to the saying 'on the ropes' which comes from the boxing ring and describes a situation where you are beaten back and close to being defeated.

Hobson's choice

Hobson's choice means no choice at all. Hobson was a real person, who lived in Cambridge in the late sixteenth and early seventeenth centuries. He was a horse-keeper but would only rent out his animals in the order he specified, rather than allowing customers to choose the one they wanted. Little did he know that this eccentricity (or was it sound business sense?) would ensure that his name lived on for centuries to come.

Hoist with your own petard

If you're unfortunate enough to be hoist with your own petard, you have been caught in your own trap or caught out by your own subterfuge. A petard was a medieval weapon that was essentially a primitive type of bomb – a casing filled with gunpowder which was attached to walls or barricades in order to blow them up. Setting and igniting a petard was a risky business, however, and it's safe to assume that a number of unfortunate petard engineers lost their lives in the explosions they themselves had set.

Hold all the cards

If you hold all the cards in a situation you have control over it, and possibly over other people who are involved as well. The saying comes from card games, and may be a reference to games in which players collect cards from their opponents until they hold them all. Alternatively it may just mean 'hold all the best cards' – either way, the player in this position will be the one to determine the outcome of the game.

Hold your horses

Meaning 'be patient' or 'wait a moment', the allusion is clear – horses that are skittish and ready to run must be held back and not allowed to dash off without a thought for safety.

If the cap fits, wear it

This expression is still very common today, although it's one of those phrases that is often shortened, with the rest being implied, as in 'If the cap fits....'. It means that if a remark or description applies to you, then you should accept it. However, it may, surprisingly, have a basis in law, and not simply fashion – in times gone by there was a law that decreed what headwear could be worn by people of different ranks. In the 1568 Bailiff's Accounts for Leominster, in Herefordshire, for example, there is an entry recording that several people were fined for wearing caps beyond their station in life! In the USA there is no record of similar laws regarding footwear, where the expression is more commonly used in the form 'If the shoe fits, wear it'.

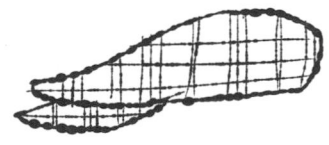

If you can't stand the heat, get out of the kitchen

This is a phrase attributed to Harry S. Truman, the thirty-third president of the United States. He is recorded as using the phrase several times, once telling his staff 'I'll stand by you, but if you can't take the heat, get out of the kitchen': in other words if you can't take the strain, don't get involved.

In a nutshell

Meaning 'stated concisely' or 'in a few words', in a nutshell is in common use today. There's an obvious suggestion that anything that fits into something so small would have to be brief, but why a nutshell? Going back many hundreds of years, we find a reference in Pliny to the whole of the Iliad being copied in a form so small that it could fit inside the shell of a walnut. This seems unlikely, given that on today's standard printer paper the text would run to 700-odd pages, and this may have been an early 'urban myth'. With modern technology, of course, creating miniature texts and miniature works of art is a whole new field.

In a pickle

References to being 'in a pickle' date back to the time of Shakespeare and all have the sense of being in a predicament or in some sort of disarray or confusion. The phrase originated in Holland where they used it in the form 'to sit in the pickle'. It's not clear when or why it came to have its figurative meaning – certainly salty water or vinegar, which are both used for preserving foods, would be quite unpleasant to sit in, so it may be that this original form inspired the analogy of being in an uncomfortable situation.

Similarly, if you're in a bit of a tricky situation you might say you are 'in a jam' – but in this instance the meaning doesn't relate to fruit spread, but to jam in the sense of 'to squeeze tightly', presumably suggesting that you've been metaphorically squeezed into a bit of a 'tight spot'.

In cahoots with

This is a very common expression meaning 'in league with'. The origin seems to be lost in the mists of time with the only suggestion put forward being that 'cahoots' is a corruption of the French word cahute, meaning cabin or hut. If that's the case, it might conjure up an image of people shut away somewhere, hatching a plot or conspiracy.

In my book

When you refer to something 'in my book' (or often in the negative 'not in my book') you're emphasising that the 'book', that is your opinion, is the 'last word' on the subject, or your definitive view of things. The saying relates to a gambling book in which a note of all bets was kept and which was therefore an undisputed record.

In the doldrums

If you're unlucky enough to be in the doldrums, you have the blues, you're depressed. The Doldrums is an area slightly north of the equator where ships were commonly becalmed. It's not actually clear whether the state of mind took its name from the geographical location, or the other way round. It may be that 'doldrums' was an old word for low spirits and that the shipping term started off as a nickname based on this, becoming in time recorded as a real place.

In the same boat

To be described as being 'in the same boat' as another person places you in the same predicament as them. The analogy is to sailors in small boats at the mercy of the elements. It wouldn't matter what rank you were. how experienced you were or even how brave you were – if the weather turned bad you were all equally at risk and your destiny would ultimately be the same.

Irons in the fire

If you have several irons in the fire you have several options. or you have several projects that you're involved in. It's hard to imagine today. with the huge variety of electrical appliances to choose from. that in order to do the ironing in the days before household electricity was the norm. you used a flat iron that had to be heated in the fire. To make the job quicker it was best to have more than one iron. so that as you used one. and it was cooling down from use. the next one could be in the fire heating up.

However. you might at times find yourself having 'too many irons in the fire'. In other words having too many projects under way. in which case you risk not being able to complete any of them successfully. In this case. the analogy suggests that your irons might get too hot. or you might lose track of which one you need to use. and risk burning your clothing.

It won't wash

This is similar in meaning to 'it won't hold water' and suggests that an explanation or excuse is far-fetched. It's believed to have arisen first in the days when patterned cloth could have a design either woven into it or printed on it. The printed cloth was cheaper but of lesser quality – and in some cases it quite literally 'wouldn't wash' as this would have washed the pattern off! So in those days the phrase referred specifically to something that had little permanence, before coming to mean more generally something that wasn't convincing.

It's an ill wind that blows nobody any good

This expression has a nautical basis: a head wind for one ship would be a tail wind for another sailing in the opposite direction. So it's come to mean that it's rare for any kind of misfortune just to have negative consequences – while things may look bad for one person, someone else might actually be benefitting from the circumstances. As with many well-known sayings, you don't always have to use the whole thing in order to be understood – often you'll hear someone saying simply 'It's an ill wind...' and leaving it at that.

Jack of all trades

It might sound like a compliment to be described as a 'Jack of all trades', being good at all sorts of things. But in fact when the phrase is used in its full form – 'Jack of all trades, master of none' – the real meaning is clearer. It's a description that is applied to someone who can turn their hand to many tasks but isn't an expert in any of them.

Jump the gun

For many years firing a gun has been the signal to start running races. A competitor who 'jumps the gun' starts running just before the gun is fired, resulting in a 'false start'. Used less literally, 'jumping the gun' can mean starting out on something before the appointed time or jumping to the wrong conclusion by assuming something without knowing all the facts.

Keep up with the Joneses

If you're trying to keep up with the Joneses you're trying to maintain a similar lifestyle as, or keep up appearances with, your neighbours. The saying was originally the title of a comic strip that appeared in the New York Globe in the early twentieth century. It's said that the artist, Arthur R. Momand, known professionally as 'Pop', actually based the series on his own attempts to keep up with his neighbours. Some hundred years later his ability to poke fun at himself lives on in this phrase which is still widely used.

Keep your pecker up

Meaning 'keep cheerful' or 'show courage', this phrase encourages you to hold your head up and not let it droop from despair. A 'pecker' is a beak, although applied to a person of course it means the mouth. Related to this, and with the same meaning, is 'keep your chin up'.

Keep your shirt on

In the days before we all had wardrobes full of clothes, a man might only have one or two shirts – perhaps one for work and one for 'best'. So if he was going to get into a brawl, he wouldn't risk getting his shirt dirty and would strip to the waist before getting 'stuck in'! So keeping your shirt on meant staying calm and avoiding a fight, and still today means 'don't get worked up'. You might also tell someone to 'keep their hair on' – this seems not to have any literal basis, but is just a humorous 'copy-cat' phrase.

Kick into touch

If a ball is 'kicked into touch' during a football match it goes out of play. So from this we get the metaphorical sense of something being over and done with, or not up for further discussion, once it's kicked into touch. It's also a slang term for 'dumping' or 'chucking' a boyfriend or girlfriend!

Kick the bucket

A light-hearted euphemism for dying. 'kick the bucket' actually doesn't relate
in any way to the modern-day meaning of bucket. The bucket in question was
a wooden frame (so named from the French word buquet, or beam) on which
slaughtered animals were suspended. Whilst being hung up, or when suffering a
spasm after slaughter, the animal could swing upwards and kick the bucket from
which it was hanging.

Kill two birds with one stone

The meaning is fairly clear – by killing two birds with one
stone you are accomplishing two things with one action.
The saying appears in various forms in other countries,
including the Italian 'catch two pigeons with one bean' and
the German 'swat two flies at once'. If you are in Russia,
however, you 'kill two hares with a single blow'.

Knock the spots off

In the late nineteenth century, skilled marksmen would demonstrate their
expertise by lining up playing cards and aiming to knock out the spots on them.
From this comes the term we now use, meaning to do something much better
than someone else, or to beat someone 'hands down'. Hands down, incidentally,
comes from horse racing and was a term used when a jockey was so far ahead

in a race that he could drop his hands, relax his grip on the reins and still win comfortably.

Know your onions

If you know your onions you know what you're talking about. But why onions? It's thought that the phrase may come from the name of one or other nineteenth-century Mr Onions – either C.T. Onions, editor of the Oxford English Dictionary, or S.G. Onions, who invented a set of coins to be used as teaching aids for children. But in fact it's equally likely just to be a nonsense phrase and that onions were picked (metaphorically speaking) at random.

Similarly, if you 'know the ropes' you're very well informed about whatever it is you're doing. The derivation of this phrase is clearer – like many expressions which have become commonplace, it's originally a nautical term. In the days of sailing ships it was vital for a sailor to understand the rigging, and how to handle the ropes, so when a new recruit had mastered this he 'knew the ropes' and had enough knowledge to handle the ship safely.

Knuckle under

There was an old custom that in the course of an argument, if you were defeated you would knock at the underside of the table with your knuckles to acknowledge that you were submitting. From this we get 'knuckle under' meaning 'to give in'.

If you 'knuckle down', of course, that's much more positive, and implies that you are getting down to work. This phrase comes from the game of marbles where traditionally the marble would be held in a crooked index finger and flicked with the thumb – in order to steady the hand for this movement the hand was placed knuckles down on the playing surface.

Land of nod

If you're off to the land of nod, you're falling asleep. The original usage was literal – the Land of Nod was the place to which Cain was exiled after killing his brother Abel, and we can assume this experience was probably less pleasant than having a good nap. But the obvious pun on the word 'nod' as in 'nodding off', when the head slumps forward as you fall asleep, led to this expression.

Laugh like a drain

In general this has come to be one of many expressions that mean to laugh a lot or uncontrollably, such as 'laugh your head off' (which hopefully has no literal origin). Strictly speaking, however, this particular phrase means to laugh noisily or coarsely, presumably like water gurgling down a drain.

Laugh up your sleeve

Whether you could do this literally rather depends on what kind of sleeves you have. But in years gone by, it would often have been possible to discreetly hide your expression by covering your face with the flowing, wide sleeve of a garment. From this comes the expression 'to laugh up your sleeve' which has the meaning of laughing to yourself, often suggesting that you are laughing at someone's misfortune or have managed to trick or deceive someone.

Let the cat out of the bag

This is a companion saying to the expression 'pig in a poke'. Unscrupulous market traders would sometimes have a young pig on display, alongside others tied in sacks. However, the sacks would in reality sometimes contain cats or puppies. So anyone who bought a pig in a poke (sack) was entering into a blind bargain and didn't know for sure what they would get. They might even find they had been 'sold a pup'! But a purchaser canny enough to check what was in the sack, by opening it, might 'let the cat out of the bag', in other words let the secret out.

Let your hair down

Meaning relax, enjoy yourself and lose your inhibitions, who wouldn't relish the occasional opportunity to let their hair down? Although this is a much-used expression, as with many phrases, it has long since lost its original meaning. It comes from the days when women always wore their hair pinned or tied up and it wasn't 'proper' to let it down in public. However in the privacy of their own homes, women probably welcomed the chance to let their hair down and worry less about the expected social graces of the day.

Level pegging

'Level pegging' is a scoring term from the card game of cribbage. The game has a unique wooden scoring board on which pegs are placed. When the players' scores are equal and their pegs are side by side on the board, they are on 'level pegging'. In its metaphorical sense, two people on a level pegging are matched equally in their abilities and/or achievements.

Cribbage also gave us the expression 'peg out', one of many euphemisms for dying. First applied to the death of humans or animals, in time it also came to be used to describe 'mechanical' deaths, for example 'my car pegged out'. The reference is to the end of a game of cribbage when a player 'pegs out' the last holes.

Level playing field

In any kind of ball game it makes sense for the playing field to be level, but despite the fact that ball games have been played for centuries, the figurative use of this term is a relatively recent one, apparently dating only from the late twentieth century. The expression is often used in business or politics to suggest even-handedness or fair competition, with no advantage being shown to either side.

Lick into shape

To make something presentable, you might say that you have to 'lick it into shape'. People can equally be licked into shape, as might dogs that require training. The phrase dates back many centuries, to medieval times, when it was widely believed that bear cubs were born shapeless and had to be made into baby bears by the licking of their mothers. The phrase exists in a slightly different form in France where someone who is a bit of a tearaway (with the implication being that their upbringing is to blame) is described as 'a badly licked bear'.

Live the life of Riley

We'd all like to live the life of Riley – a nice happy, easy life with anything we wanted available to us. There are numerous theories about who Riley (or Reilly) was, but the saying may have originated with a late nineteenth-century American song called 'Is That Mr Reilly?' in which the hero describes his plans for the life he would like to live when he makes his fortune.

LONG IN the TOOTH

If someone's getting a bit long in the tooth they are simply getting old. Although people's teeth can look longer as they grow old and their gums recede, the origin of this saying is the equine world, as horses' teeth continue to grow throughout their lives, and are used as an indicator of the age of the animal.

Mad as a hatter /
Mad as a March hare

In Lewis Carroll's Alice's Adventures in Wonderland, the Cheshire Cat tells Alice that she can go in one of two directions, to meet either a hatter or a March hare and advises 'Visit either you like: they're both mad.' Carroll of course didn't invent the concept of the mad hatter or the mad March hare – both would have been as familiar to his readers as they are to us today, and both have a basis in fact.

Hat makers were prone to disorders of the nervous system and behavioural and mood swings as a result of their use of mercury (which is highly toxic) in the hat-making process. This probably gave rise to the common notion that those who worked in this trade were, to some degree or another, 'mad.' As for hares, March is the month in which they breed and at this time they indulge in elaborate and energetic courtship displays. Leaping and running about wildly, the hares appear to be behaving out of character, looking to an observer as if they are in some way mad.

Make a bee-line for

If you make a bee-line for something you head straight for it, without any deviation. Incredibly, bees are able to do this when they are given information by a forager bee on the source of nectar. The forager will return to the hive and perform what's known as a 'waggle dance', which is sophisticated enough to tell the other bees in which direction to fly and for what distance.

Might as well be hanged for a sheep as a lamb

It was only in the nineteenth century that the theft of a sheep or a lamb in some parts of the country ceased to be punishable by death. Two centuries earlier the saying 'might as well be hanged for a sheep as a lamb' was already a much-quoted proverb, implying that if the consequences are the same, you might as well do something drastic or aim for something of higher value.

Mind your Ps and Qs

Meaning 'mind your manners' or 'be on your best behaviour', this is an expression with a whole host of possible origins. From the simple theory that 'Ps and Qs' is shorthand for 'pleases and thank-yous' to the suggestion that Ps and Qs were used to tally up drinks bought 'on the slate' by the pint or quart; from the argument that it was advice to children or printers not to confuse the similar lower-case letters to the conjecture that it was an instruction by French dancing teachers to mind the pieds (feet) and queues (wigs) when dancing – well, as another well-known saying goes – 'you pays your money and you takes your choice'!

Move the goalposts

If you 'move the goalposts', figuratively, you are changing agreed rules or conditions after something has started – and probably doing so to someone else's disadvantage. The saying alludes, predictably enough, to sports such as football and rugby, where although there are no known records of anyone physically doing this during a game, the meaning is clear – if you did manage to do it, it would certainly be rather unfair on the attacking team, who then wouldn't know where to aim the ball!

Nail your colours to the mast

Military or naval flags ('colours') are hoisted to the top of a flagpole and secured in place by lines. However, there was always the risk that in a battle, these could be shot away. This could be demoralising to your troops, especially as lowering your colours was a signal of surrender. To avoid this risk, colours could be nailed to the mast – so not only were they safe from gunfire, but they also couldn't be lowered in submission or defeat. Therefore, 'nailing your colours to the mast' makes your intentions clear – you're prepared to fight on to the bitter end, and you'll never admit defeat.

Neck and neck

A 'neck' is one of the officially recognised measures used in horse racing to estimate distance between runners. The others are 'nose', 'head', 'length' and 'distance'. When horses are described as being 'neck and neck' they are very close together, in fact virtually side by side. So the phrase has come to be used to describe any two competitors or contenders with little to show between them, whether they are physically close in a race of some sort or simply have the same score in a competition. Why 'neck' became the term favoured for this, as opposed to one of the other options, isn't known – perhaps 'nose and nose' just sounded too silly!

Neither fish nor fowl

Something that is neither one thing nor another and so is in effect useless. is referred to as being 'neither fish nor fowl'. The full expression is 'neither fish. flesh (or fowl). nor good red herring'. The saying dates from the Middle Ages when specific foods were eaten by the various classes of society. Fish was eaten by the clergy. flesh (or fowl) was the food of the common man. and red herrings were the fare of paupers.

Nest egg

A nest egg is an amount of money saved for future use. It's thought that the term derives from the practice of putting a false egg in a hen's nest to encourage it to lay more. Whether the original meaning was that this figurative 'nest egg' would encourage further savings. or whether it simply meant something that you put by to retrieve at a later date isn't clear. but nowadays it does tend to suggest a lump sum put by 'for a rainy day'.

New brooms sweep clean

It may not be literally true that a new broom is more efficient. but the implication of this saying is that someone new to a role will be very keen and may want to impose changes or get rid of wasteful practices. It may be that they are trying to make their role or their organisation more efficient. or it may simply be that they want to 'make their mark'.

Night on the tiles

If you've had a night on the tiles, you've been out partying and generally having a good time. It's thought that the expression refers to the night-time activities of cats frolicking on rooftops.

While you were about it, you might have been 'painting the town red'. There are all sorts of theories about the origin of this one – from a real nineteenth-century incident where a group of young aristocrats actually painted some of the buildings red in the town of Melton Mowbray for a prank, to suggestions that it is a reference to red-light districts. These days, though, whatever the origin of the phrase, it simply means going on a bit of a spree, and there's no suggestion that you're doing anything illegal or immoral in the process.

Nineteen to the dozen

These days it's most common to hear this phrase as part of the expression 'talking nineteen to the dozen' and the suggestion is that someone who does this is talking very quickly – in a sense trying to fit nineteen words into the time it should take to say twelve. However, this sense of speed came into being from the early days of steam engines, notably those used to power pumps in mines. A steam engine going 'nineteen to the dozen' was pumping 19,000 gallons of water for every twelve bushels of coal it burned. So in those days, used in its literal sense, something going 'nineteen to the dozen' was working at optimum efficiency.

Nineteenth hole

This will be a term familiar to golfers, but for those who know only the basics, a reference to a nineteenth hole might be puzzling. Surely a golf course commonly has either nine or eighteen holes? The nineteenth hole, however, is not for sinking a ball – it's for sinking a post-play drink, and is the name given by players to the club bar.

Nip in the bud

If you nip something in the bud, you're stopping it from going any further. The term dates back to the seventeenth century and comes of course from the garden. A bud might be nipped by frost or pests, or you might pinch buds off by hand, and this prevents the plant from growing any more at that point.

No names, no pack-drill

Meaning 'keep mum', say nothing and no one will be punished, this saying has a military origin. Now obsolete, one form of punishment for misdemeanours in the British Army used to be that the offender would be made to undertake drill (exercise) in full kit and with a heavy pack. But if the offender's name was not known, he couldn't be punished.

Not for all the tea in China

Although it dates from the nineteenth century, and seems to have been coined in Australia, this is a phrase that is still very common throughout the English-speaking world. Meaning 'not under any circumstances', it's a very obvious reference to the fact that China produces a significant amount of the world's tea.

A related expression dating from around the same time is 'not my cup of tea', meaning 'not to my liking', although the phrase was originally used in a positive way, with 'my cup of tea' being more often than not a description of a person you particularly liked. Either way, these sayings would have been easy for anyone to understand, given that tea was, and still is, such a popular drink.

Nothing to write home about

As the writing of letters becomes a dying art, this saying could easily be re-phrased as 'nothing to email about' or even 'nothing to text about'! In its figurative sense it has little to do with letters themselves, but is just a general way of suggesting that there is nothing remarkable about a person or thing that merits particular comment. The phrase is found in English going back centuries, but became popular during the First World War when soldiers could spend long periods awaiting battle orders and then quite literally had nothing to write home about.

NUTTY AS A FRUIT CAKE

This is a slang, yet relatively light-hearted, expression suggesting that someone is 'bonkers' or a bit eccentric. The origin is uncertain, but nuts seem to have gained an association with craziness for some reason, as in the simple phrase 'he's nuts'. As fruit cakes generally also contain a lot of nuts, it can only be assumed that 'nutty as a fruit cake' was a way of saying that someone was very nutty indeed! Of course there can be a more positive connotation of 'nuts', meaning that you're really enthusiastic, or 'crazy', about something or someone, as in 'he's nuts about his new girlfriend'.

Off the cuff

An off the cuff remark is a spontaneous one. No one is quite sure why this should be, however. There is a theory that in days gone by tradesmen used to make notes on their shirt cuffs (which would have been easier in the days when collars and cuffs were separate from the body of the shirt itself) or that after-dinner speakers were prone to using their cuffs to jot down 'spontaneous' witticisms that occurred to them before they stood up to make a speech.

Off your own bat

This was originally a cricketing term. Although runs could be scored in many ways, including 'extra' runs (for example when a fielder threw the ball at the stumps and missed, giving the batsman time to run again), it was the runs scored 'off his own bat' that really gave the batsman the most satisfaction. So the expression has come to refer to achieving something by your own exertions, or in a more general sense to using your own initiative and 'taking things into your own hands'.

On a sticky wicket

This is another saying that has come into our language from the cricket pitch. A sticky wicket is hard to play on: rain-soaked, but fast drying, it can make the ball break sharply and rise abruptly. So you need to keep your wits about you in these playing conditions. Similarly, in a figurative sense, if you're on a sticky wicket you might be in a tricky or awkward situation so you need to 'tread carefully'.

On a wing and a prayer

If you're trying to achieve something 'on a wing and a prayer' you're struggling against the odds but you just might manage it. The saying originated during the Second World War. Whether or not it was ever actually spoken by a pilot of a stricken aircraft, there was certainly a line in a film that referred to a plane coming in 'on one wing and a prayer' and this seems to have inspired the 1943 song Coming In on a Wing and a Prayer. From there, the phrase passed into popular usage.

On the back foot

A boxer who is in control of his fighting leads with the front foot, placing his weight on it when he lands his punches. But if his opponent begins to 'get the upper hand' and land a series of punches, he will be forced to retreat 'on the back foot'. This leads to the meaning of the expression when used metaphorically – to be forced onto the back foot means that you have to adopt a defensive posture from which it could be difficult to launch any kind of 'comeback' or counter-attack.

On the ball

When you're 'on the ball' you're alert or in control of things. Yet another sporting analogy, this comes from the need in any ball game – whether field games such as football and hockey or racket games such as tennis and squash – to 'keep your eye on the ball'. That in itself is another well-known saying, meaning to keep track of things or 'keep your wits about you'. Of course if you 'take your eye off the ball' in a game, you could be in trouble, and the same applies figuratively in other situations.

On tick

Meaning, 'on credit' – or as they say these days 'buy now pay later' – 'tick' here isn't the little symbol for correctness that we are all familiar with, but a short form of the word 'ticket', in other words the note that was written to record your debt.

On your tod

A well-used expression, meaning 'on your own', on your tod derives from rhyming slang. In this case it was 'on your Tod Sloan', the man in question being a famous jockey in the early part of the twentieth century. Many rhyming slang phrases arose from using the names of celebrities and as in this case the sayings live on, and are clearly understood, long after the people who inspired them have died and been forgotten.

ONCE IN A BLUE MOON

Something that happens very rarely can be said to occur once in a blue moon. Some say this is because very occasionally atmospheric conditions do make the moon look blue. Others cite almanacs which refer to blue moons as being either the thirteenth full moon in a calendar year, or the second full moon in a calendar month. These aren't really all that rare, but nonetheless, without having to get into a discussion on the astronomical accuracy, you can assume that when someone uses this phrase, they are referring to something that doesn't happen very often.

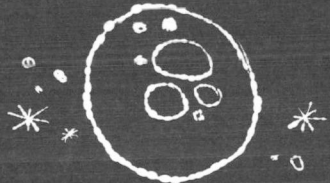

An interesting regional phrase meaning the same thing is the Lancashire expression 'once every Preston Guild'. Preston Guilds are held only once every twenty years – starting life as a kind of twelfth-century 'trade fair', the Guild is now a festival for all the people of the city. The most recent one was held in 2012.

One-horse race

Clearly, a one-horse race wouldn't be any kind of competition at all, but the saying alludes to a race where there is one clear favourite and none of the others stand a chance of beating it. From this, we get the phrase which can be applied to other situations in which one competitor is sure to win. Whether the saying is applied to a job vacancy, an election or a sporting competition, it's a 'one-horse race' if there's an outright winner before the official decision is made or the competition won.

There's another phrase with the same meaning and it's likely to also have come from the world of horse racing, and that's 'shoo-in'. If you're, say, a 'shoo-in' for a job, it means no one else stands a chance of getting it. It's likely to be a reference to 'shooing' an animal along – the suggestion being that even if the horse in question was reluctant to cross the finishing line and had to be shooed across, it would still beat all the others.

One over the eight

If you've had one over the eight, you're drunk – especially if the 'eight' refers to eight pints, as is commonly believed!

Ours not to reason why

Meaning 'it's not for us to question', this is one of those expressions that we all use, perhaps not realising that it's in fact a mis-quotation. The original, from Tennyson's poem about the disastrous Charge of the Light Brigade, was: 'Theirs not to reason why, Theirs but to do or die'. Thankfully today the phrase is rarely used in life or death situations.

Over a barrel

You might be literally draped over a barrel if you were unfortunate enough to have come close to drowning – this would help your rescuer to expel water from your lungs. Worse off than that, however, were those who were draped over a barrel in order to be beaten as a form of punishment. Either way, you're not in control of the situation and if someone has you 'over a barrel' you are at their mercy.

Over-egg the pudding

The danger of putting too much of any ingredient into a dish is a 'recipe for disaster', and in the case of eggs it is no exception. In a non-literal sense, 'to over-egg the pudding' means to wildly exaggerate or overstate your case, which figuratively could also be another 'recipe for disaster'.

Over the moon

If you're really delighted about something you might say you're 'over the moon'. The expression refers to being so excited that you could not only 'jump for joy' but go much further! The origin of this saying is likely to be the well-known nursery rhyme Hey Diddle Diddle in which it is the cow that jumps over the moon. But quite what the origins of that were, no one knows. Like many nursery rhymes, its original meaning (if it had one) is lost in the mists of time. It may simply have always been a nonsense rhyme, but the idea of jumping the moon evidently appealed and gave rise to this still-popular expression.

Pan out

When we say 'let's see how things pan out' we mean let's see how they turn out or conclude. The pans in question aren't kitchen pots and pans, but the pans used by gold prospectors who rolled gravel around in them looking for tiny fragments of gold. In those circumstances, if you 'panned out' you got a good result.

Pass muster

If you're going to 'pass muster' you're required to come up to a certain standard. The origin is the muster, or military parade, at which troops were assembled and inspected. 'Muster' entered English from the old French moustre, which in turn was derived from the Latin word monstrare, meaning 'to point out' or 'to show'.

PASS the BUCK

These days, 'passing the buck' means evading responsibility or shifting blame onto other people. When the phrase was coined in the nineteenth century, however, it had a different emphasis. In some card games a marker, known as a 'buck', was placed in front of the dealer to show who the dealer was. When it was someone else's turn to deal, the 'buck' was passed. Originally the 'buck' may have been a knife with a buck's-horn handle, a piece of buck-shot, or possibly a silver dollar, which was passed from dealer to dealer.

Related to this is the phrase 'the buck stops here'. President Harry S. Truman had a sign on his desk with these words on, making clear his pledge to take personal responsibility for the way the country was governed.

PDQ

Meaning 'pretty damn quick', this is a good example of an abbreviation that pre-dates mobile phones and texting by more than a century. The phrase was first used, in this abbreviated form at any rate, by a character in a late nineteenth-century play by Benjamin E. Woolf, entitled The Mighty Dollar. All sorts of other abbreviations are used by the same character, but for some reason this one moved into popular usage while others are long since forgotten.

In a similar vein, of course, is the abbreviation 'asap' – as soon as possible. This one, however, is sometimes pronounced as a word rather than spelt out letter by letter. Another abbreviated phrase in common use – but this time with no known explanation – is the expression 'on the QT' meaning 'on the quiet'.

Pie in the sky

When this phrase was popularised in the early years of the twentieth century it formed part of a clear political message. In 1911 a militant Trade Union song book, Songs of the Workers, was published and included among its titles The Preacher and the Slave by Joe Hill, which contained the verse:

You will eat, by and by,
In that glorious land above the sky;
Work and pray, live on hay,
You'll get pie in the sky when you die.

Since then 'pie in the sky' has meant the 'good time' or the 'good things' that are promised but which never come or are never realised in this life.

Pies also feature in other well-known sayings such as 'As easy as pie' (which presumably means as easy as eating a pie rather than making one). 'Eat humble pie' (see page 48) or 'Have your finger in (too) many pies' (be involved in (too) many different interests).

Piece of cake

Something straightforward to do can be described as a 'piece of cake'. This seems to be an American expression. but was popularised during the Second World War by the RAF. It's a simple allusion. as far as anyone knows. to cutting and eating a slice of cake.

Pipe dream

Across many different cultures down the centuries it was common to smoke opium pipes. The effect was often to give the user vivid dreams. which might be weird or fantastical. and which. it is said. inspired great works of literature and art. From this we get the expression 'pipe dreams'. but the figurative meaning refers to wild dreams in the sense of unrealistic hopes and fantasies.

Piping hot

When reheating food. we are often told to ensure that it is 'piping hot throughout' and we accept this as a clear instruction that the food should be very hot indeed. The 'piping' in this phrase is not. as you might think. anything to do with the Scottish ceremony of piping in the haggis. nor anything to do with piping food aboard a ship. In fact. it's simply an allusion to the whistling. hissing sound made by steam escaping from very hot food. and the phrase has been in use for centuries. Chaucer uses it in his Miller's Tale. when he refers to the delicious-sounding 'waffles piping hot out of the fire'.

Play for time

The end of a cricket match doesn't necessarily mean victory for one team and defeat for another. A draw is a possible third outcome and this can be achieved by a team that uses the appropriate tactics and so avoids defeat – in order to do this the team must keep batting until time runs out. Hence the expression 'playing for time'. which implies that the batting team have given up playing for runs. but are just batting cautiously and defensively so that they can continue batting until the end of the game. As a metaphor. 'playing for time' suggests using any kind of delaying tactic to stave off defeat or failure. or to 'buy time' until things go your way.

The same tactic is sometimes known as 'stonewalling' and this expression too has entered the language in a figurative sense. meaning exactly the same thing – adopting delaying tactics.

Play your cards close to your chest

This saying comes from games of cards. where a player who was especially cautious might hold his or her cards quite literally close to their chest. so that other players couldn't see them. Figuratively. then. it has come to mean being secretive about your plans.

Whilst playing your cards close to your chest it might also help to have a 'poker face' – that is. an expressionless face which doesn't give anything away. If you've played your cards close to your chest. and you are then able to outdo someone. especially with an unexpected flourish. at that point you could be said to be 'playing your trump card!

Pull a fast one

Yet another saying that originates in the world of cricket. 'pulling a fast one' was a reference to bowling an unexpectedly fast ball. Whilst perfectly within the rules of the game. pulling a fast one was sometimes seen as not the gentlemanly thing to do and the phrase has now come to encompass the meaning of achieving something by slightly dubious means.

PULL the WOOL OVER SOMEONE'S EYES

This expression meaning 'to deceive' comes from the days when wigs were the fashion. They were commonly known as 'wool' because of the resemblance to a sheep's fleece. especially wigs with tight curls. Therefore. to pull the wool over someone's eyes would be to stop them seeing what was happening around them. and so to deceive them.

Pull your leg

If you have your leg pulled, you're the victim of some kind of teasing or practical joke. The origin of the phrase is uncertain but it may refer to tripping someone up for fun (or for more sinister reasons, such as robbery) and it dates back to at least the nineteenth century.

More recent is the saying you might use to make it known that you won't be caught out or tricked – 'pull the other one'. In its full form this was 'pull the other one, it's got bells on', perhaps simply suggesting that if the joker did that, they'd at least get something out of it.

Pull your punches

Boxers who 'pull their punches' deliberately lessen the force of their blows by pulling their fists back just before impact, to spare their opponents the full force of the attack. Metaphorically, people who pull their punches in other situations hold back to some extent to spare the feelings of someone else. It's another phrase that's perhaps more frequently used in the negative form, when you want to suggest that someone has not been tactful, or has been particularly blunt about something, as in 'he didn't pull any punches'.

Pull your weight

This is a rowing term – 'pulling your weight' means putting all the strength of your body into your strokes to move the boat along. Anyone not pulling their weight is a drag on the rest of the crew. Metaphorically speaking, then, in any kind of team endeavour, it's important that each person pulls their weight in order not to hinder the efforts of others.

Punch-drunk

After repeated blows to the head, a boxer might show signs of being 'punch-drunk' – it's a form of concussion that leaves the boxer with damage to the brain and results in unsteadiness and mild confusion or disorientation. In its figurative usage, anyone who is punch-drunk is in a state of bewilderment or confusion or is dazed – although in this case not by actual blows but by having too much to take in, in any sense, from exciting news to over-work.

Push the boat out

This suggests an act of generosity – by pushing the boat out you're often treating others, maybe on a special occasion. It clearly originates in nautical circles, but whether it's a simple allusion to needing to get a group of people together to literally push a boat off shore and into the water (perhaps treating them to a drink afterwards to thank them) or whether it referred to a celebration held prior to a voyage, isn't known for sure.

Put a sock in it

This impolite way of asking someone to quieten down is said to come from the days of wind-up gramophones, where the sound came out through a horn. In lieu of a volume control, it was said that a sock was the most efficient way of muffling the sound.

Put the cart before the horse

In other languages, this is often used in the form 'put the oxen before the plough' – either way it carries the same meaning, suggesting doing things in the wrong order.

Horses also feature in the saying 'locking the stable door after the horse has bolted', in other words doing something too late for it to make any difference.

Put the kibosh on

Meaning put an end or a stop to something, 'put the kibosh on' may come from the Yiddish word kabas meaning 'to suppress'. It's equally likely, though, that the origin is the Irish cie bas, or 'cap of death' (as worn by judges pronouncing a death sentence), which has a similar pronunciation to 'kibosh' as we say it today.

Put through your paces

If you're thinking of buying a horse, you'll want to see it 'put through its paces' first – the paces being walk, trot, canter and gallop – to see how well it performs. The same expression is used in any situation where someone or something is being assessed.

Put your best foot forward

Now here's an odd expression. As any pedant will tell you, if you're talking about people, who only have two feet, this saying isn't grammatically correct. You can't have 'the best' of only two, but you can have 'the better'. Shakespeare knew this, when he wrote 'make haste; the better foot before' in King John. But pedantry aside, the expression has been used in its current form since the seventeenth century, and means to start out on a task with enthusiasm, to try your best or to set out to make a good impression.

Pyrrhic victory

'Victory' sounds unambiguously positive, but if you win a Pyrrhic victory it means that the achievement of your victory or success is outweighed by the personal cost. In 279 BC Pyrrhus, the King of Epirus in Greece, led a sizeable army against the Romans at the battle of Asculum. Although his forces won, the cost in casualties was so great that Pyrrhus has gone down in history for his wry comment 'One more such victory and we are lost.'

Raining cats and dogs

We're all familiar with this saying, referring to very heavy rain, but there's a lot of debate about its origin. It seems that there are two strong contenders for the source. One is rooted in mythology: witches, who were known to disguise themselves as cats, rode on storms, while dogs and wolves were attendants of the Norse god Odin, the god of storms.

The other explanation is a little more down to earth, quite literally, and that is that in the days when drainage was poor and sewers non-existent, heavy storms and floods would often result in all sorts of disgusting debris being washed down the streets – including quite possibly the bodies of dead animals. Although they hadn't actually dropped from the sky, the impression might be that they had arrived with the storm.

Other rain-related sayings include: 'It never rains but it pours' (meaning that when one bad thing happens, others tend to follow); 'Taking a rain check' (originally a deferred ticket to a US baseball game that was rained off, now used to signify any promise to accept an invitation at another time); and 'Come rain or shine' (meaning whatever the weather).

Rank and file

The 'rank and file' are the ordinary members of an organisation or association, excluding the group leaders. This is another saying that comes from a military context, where soldiers in rank stood in rows and those in file stood in columns, one behind the other. Taken together, 'rank and file' came to be used to distinguish ordinary soldiers from commissioned officers. As an aside, chess pieces are also described as being in ranks and files, echoing the military usage.

Red herring

A smoked and salted herring turns a reddish colour, so that takes care of the literal meaning. But why has this come to be used to describe a false clue or trail? One popular theory has it that these particular fish were drawn across the countryside to set scented trails for hunting hounds, diverting them from their true prey. There certainly is evidence of trails being laid in this way as far back as the seventeenth century. But it's not clear why this would have been done (unless it was an early form of hunt sabotage, which in the context of the times seems unlikely).

Maybe the point was that such trails were used to train the dogs, not divert them – and the modern meaning of a diversion or deceit arises from the fact that from the dogs' point of view, it was indeed a false trail, with no catch at the end of it.

Red-letter day

'Red-letter days' are days to be looked forward to. when something special or exciting is going to take place. The meaning was originally quite literal: in bygone times saints' days and important Christian feast days were printed in red ink on the church calendar to distinguish them from other days in the church year which were printed in black.

Red sky at night

The full saying is. of course. 'Red sky at night. shepherds delight: red sky in the morning. shepherds warning'. In the days before accurate weather forecasting using modern technology. those who worked the land or sailed the seas came to rely on traditional wisdom when it came to predicting the weather for the day ahead. In this instance. the saying is reasonably accurate: after a red sunset. a good day can generally be expected to follow and after a red sunrise it might be wise to dress for a wetter day.

Red tape

We use 'red tape' as a description of excessive or unnecessary bureaucracy because red tape is used used by government officials and lawyers to tie up bundles of documents.

Ride roughshod over

Those who 'ride roughshod' over others act with absolutely no thought for their feelings or interests. The expression originated among battlefield cavalry units of days gone by. in which horses were sometimes fitted with special shoes which had sharp projections such as nails. These would prevent them from slipping during a charge but also had a far more sinister use in inflicting terrible wounds on the foot soldiers they fought against. who could be horribly injured if they were unfortunate enough to be ridden over. Although the literal meaning has long since ceased to apply. the saying is still frequently used in its figurative sense.

Right-hand man

As the senior assistant a 'right-hand man' was accorded pride of place over other servants and traditionally this was on his master's right-hand side. In this position he was better placed to fend off attack with the use of his sword. Nowadays of course. the term is used to suggest all sorts of duties more mundane than fighting off attackers – anyone from an efficient administrator to a close friend might be described as a 'right-hand man'. as indeed might a woman!

Ring the changes

In traditional English bell-ringing changes are rung using all the combinations of a set of bells. This has extended into everyday speech as an allusion to repeating the same thing. or re-using resources. in a different way.

Rob Peter to pay Paul

These days, with credit more readily available than ever, it's likely that some people with debts find themselves 'robbing Peter to pay Paul', in other words paying off one debt by incurring another. No one really knows who the Peter and Paul are in this expression – there are theories that they are churches, or that the names are a reference to Saints Peter and Paul, but it's equally possible that the names have no particular significance.

Run rings round

If you run rings round someone you are defeating or outclassing them easily in some kind of sport or competition. The origin of this phrase lies in the sports of fox-hunting and hare-coursing, where the prey would run in circles trying to outwit and escape the hunting dogs.

Salt away

Before refrigeration was widely available, preserving food in brine or barrels of salt was a common method of setting aside provisions for future use. The food preserved in this way could be used over the winter, or on long sea voyages, when fresh food wasn't available. The value of doing this gave rise to the expression to 'salt away', meaning to set aside for use at a later date. It can apply to anything that is stored up, but the expression is often used to describe money, in which case the implication is that it's hidden away.

Salt of the earth

Salt was a vital commodity in the ancient world. Roman soldiers received part of their pay as a salarium, an allowance with which they bought salt: the English word 'salary' is derived from this.

Salt was used to preserve food as well as season it, and the saying 'salt of the earth' received its ultimate endorsement when Christ used the term to describe his disciples in the Sermon on the Mount: 'Ye are the salt of the earth.' From this point on, anyone described as the salt of the earth could reasonably regard themselves as among the best of mankind.

Sandwich short of a picnic

If you describe someone as 'a sandwich short of a picnic' you're saying that they're 'intellectually challenged' – but in a light-hearted way. You might also use the term 'one brick short of a load', although there are many other similar sayings and many regional variations. A comparable phrase from America is to say that some has 'fifty cards in the pack' – of course a full deck has fifty-two cards so the implication is the same – there's something missing or the person is 'not all there'.

There are also many expressions to convey the same meaning that use the format 'not the...' – as in 'not the brightest button in the box', 'not the sharpest knife in the drawer' and so forth.

Save your bacon

There are several ideas about why this expression conveys the idea of saving yourself from injury or harm. The first is based on the importance of bacon as the principal meat that was salted and preserved for the lean winter months. A diligent housewife would take steps to prevent such a store being tampered with, or raided, to ensure her family was catered for until spring.

The second explanation is based on the idea that the Anglo-Saxon word for 'back' was baec; therefore to 'save your bacon', it is thought, was to literally save your back from a thrashing.

The third alternative is that in medieval times, 'bacon' described any flesh from the animal and thus came to be a slang term for the body. So by that definition, 'saving your bacon' was quite literally saving your body from harm.

Scot free

With many Scots today keen to have independence for their country, 'scot free' could have all sorts of implications. But of course it simply means getting away with something, whether that's a payment or a punishment. It doesn't have a direct connection with Scotland, either. The word 'scot' is a corruption of skat, a Scandinavian word for a tax or payment. As no one likes paying taxes, getting off scot free has been a desirable goal for many centuries!

Send to Coventry

In its figurative sense, being sent to Coventry means being ignored or ostracised. It's believed that the expression derives from a time when being sent to Coventry was a literal punishment. The time was the English Civil War, and the story goes that Cromwell sent a group of Royalist soldiers there to be imprisoned. Being parliamentary supporters, the local people refused to have anything to do with them. Any local woman seen talking to one of the captured soldiers would also be shunned, so from this period in history we get the meaning that we are all familiar with today.

Set the Thames on fire

This is one of those sayings that tends to be used in the negative, for example 'He'll never set the Thames on fire'. Interestingly, the expression exists in many other European countries too, in which case you'd refer, for example, to the Seine, the Rhine or the Tiber. Whatever the name of the river, the meaning is the same, suggesting that the poor fellow in question won't make much of a mark in life, or do anything memorable. The origin is obscure – it may be a simple metaphorical reference to something that's impossible (setting fire to water) or it may hark back to the great firework celebrations that were held (and indeed still are) on the water to mark great occasions.

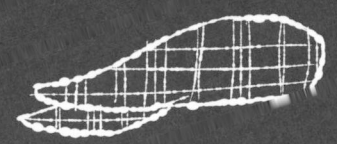

SET YOUR CAP AT SOMEONE

If you set your cap at someone, you're usually a woman trying to attract the attentions of a man. It's clear to see that in the days when women never ventured out without a hat or bonnet of some sort, wearing your best headgear, and setting it at the most flattering angle, would be just one of the ways you might try to impress potential suitors.

Shanks's pony

Shanks's pony (or in the US more commonly shanks's mare) isn't an animal at all of course. If you travel by shanks's pony you are walking. The origin is simply a reference to the shank (the shinbone) and the phrase seems to have been coined in Scotland in the eighteenth century, where it was also sometimes given as shanks's nag.

Shell-shocked

If you're shell-shocked you are in a state of shock because of something awful, particularly something sudden or unexpected, that has happened to you. 'Shell-shock' was the description given to the psychological trauma suffered by soldiers in the First World War in response to the horrors of battle.

Shilly-shally

If you're shilly-shallying over a decision, you're dithering (or if you're in Scotland you're probably 'swithering'!). The most likely origin of this phrase is the self-questioning 'Shall I...?' From the pondering 'Shall I, shall I not?', the phrase seems to have mutated into the light-hearted 'shilly-shally' that we are familiar with today.

Shoot your bolt

In medieval archery a 'bolt' was the short blunt arrow fired from a crossbow. Although powerful and accurate. crossbows were cumbersome weapons to reload and as a result had a far slower rate of fire than the longbow. With only one bolt to shoot at a time. an archer who had shot his bolt had nothing with which to attack (or possibly defend himself) until he reloaded the next. From this we get the present-day meaning of 'shooting your bolt'. to have tried your utmost. or done all you can.

Short end of the stick

If you're the unlucky person who gets the short end of the stick. you're the one who's come off worst in something competitive or in a bargain or deal of some sort. But this is another one of those expressions that we use without stopping to think about. How can a stick have a 'short end'? So this saying has be to classified as one with no clear origin. although it's meaning is clear and it is widely used.

Of course you might also find yourself getting 'the wrong end of the stick'. Originally this meant the same thing – getting the 'raw deal' – but somewhere around the nineteenth century the meaning seems to have changed. and now it means you've misunderstood something.

SHOW A LEG

Meaning 'get up' or more generally 'get a move on', it's said that this phrase originated in the days when sailors' wives or girlfriends were allowed to stay with them on board ship. Allegedly the waking call 'show a leg' was an instruction to do exactly that – those legs that were too shapely to belong to sailors were clearly a sign that there was a 'lady friend' in the bed and she would be left alone! Whether or not this is true, it's a nice idea – but it may simply be that 'show a leg' is a way of saying 'show me that you're awake and moving' which as any parent of a teenager will tell you is the first step in what can be a long process of persuading someone to get out of a nice warm cosy bed.

Since Pontius was a pilot

Meaning 'since time immemorial', this is an expression coined in the RAF, predictably making the most of the pun on the name of Pontius Pilate, the Roman prefect who ordered the execution of Jesus Christ. Related to this is the US variant 'when Christ was a corporal'.

Other expressions that mean something similar include 'since Adam was a lad', 'since Methuselah was a boy', or again from the US and Canada, 'since Hector was a pup' (Hector as in the Trojan War and 'pup' as in the sense of a youngster). You might also refer to something that has been the case 'for donkey's years' (probably a corrupted form of rhyming slang from donkey's ears – years) or for 'yonks' (and no, no one knows what a yonk is!).

Skirt round

If you skirt round a subject, you're avoiding the main issue. The meaning of 'skirt' here is an old one, and nothing to do with clothing. It comes from the hunting field, where a hound that cuts corners, instead of following the exact line of the scent, is known as a 'skirt', and a hunter who goes round an obstacle rather than over or through it is known as a 'skirter'.

Sleep like a top

If you are lucky enough to sleep like a top, you sleep very soundly. There are two possible sources of this well-used phrase. One alludes to a spinning top which appears to be completely still when it is spinning fastest. But it's also possible that the expression comes from the Italian 'ei dorme come un topo', which means 'he sleeps like a mouse' – perhaps a reference to the famously sleepy dormouse.

You might also say that you 'sleep like a log' or 'sleep like a baby'. The 'log' reference seems also to suggest something, or someone, that doesn't move all night. The 'baby' analogy is slightly more controversial. Babies certainly do sleep incredibly deeply – if and when they sleep. But anyone who has had a colicky or restless baby would probably not choose this particular term to describe a good night's sleep!

Soft soap

To 'soft soap' someone is to flatter them or 'butter them up'. Probably a reference to the froth and smoothness of fine soaps (as opposed to the harsh versions that were commonly used for many years), the expression suggests being especially nice to someone to gain what you want.

Sour grapes

This expression refers to the sulkiness or bitterness you might display when something doesn't go your way. It comes from the Aesop fable (dating from the sixth century BC) of the fox. The fox failed to reach the grapes he craved. so he comforted himself by saying that they weren't ripe anyway.

Speak of the devil

Another saying that's rarely used in its full form. this saying was originally 'Speak of the devil and he'll appear' – a very real belief held by many in times past when people believed that talking of bad things would make them happen. (Today we still talk of 'tempting fate' so we're probably just as superstitious as our ancestors.) Now it's far less threatening and is simply used when you're talking about someone and at that moment they turn up.

Spick and span

The original expression was 'spick and span new'. meaning brand new. but these days we tend to use this phrase to mean more generally neat and clean. It comes from the world of sailing ships: a spick was a nail or spike used in ship-building and a span was a chip of wood. So a brand new ship would have visible spicks and spans. The first recorded use of the phrase in its form 'spick and span' is found in the diary of Samuel Pepys from 1665. when he referred to 'My Lady Batten ... with new spicke and span white shoes'.

Spill the beans

To 'spill the beans' is to let slip information which would otherwise have been kept secret, or to give away a plot under pressure to divulge it. One explanation places the origin of the phrase in ancient Greece, where beans of two different colours were used in secret ballots: a white bean signified 'yes; a brown bean counted as a 'no' vote. When all votes had been cast, the beans were counted in secret, but if the beans were accidentally spilt the result could be seen at a glance and the vote was void.

Another line of thought follows the idea that some fortune-tellers use beans instead of crystal balls or tea leaves. They rely on spilling beans from a cup and then interpreting the future from the pattern made by them.

It may be simpler than either of those explanations, however. There has long been an expression meaning to know what's what – 'know your beans' – so if you know your beans it may be possible for you to spill them.

Spit feathers

For years, if you were 'spitting feathers' you were extremely thirsty. It's not clear where the phrase originated but the meaning is fairly obvious – your mouth is dry. In more recent times, however, the phrase seems to have acquired a second meaning – very angry (similar to the expression 'spitting blood'). Likewise, there is no clear explanation for this, but if someone tells you they're 'spitting feathers' it might be a good idea to clarify what they mean!

Spoil the ship for a ha'porth of tar

This is something you really wouldn't want to do – spoil something just for the sake of economising on something small, such as a ha'porth (half a penny's worth) of tar. Despite appearances, this expression is not one that owes its origins to life at sea – it's rooted in agricultural practices, and the 'ship' in question is just a dialect form of the word 'sheep'.

When sheep were injured, their wounds would be sealed with tar to prevent infection, so what the expression is saying is that it isn't worth risking the loss of a valuable sheep just to save a few pence on something that could prevent it from dying.

From the same source we get the saying 'tarred with the same brush' – all the sheep would be treated at the same time and in the same way, and thus literally tarred with the same brush. Used figuratively, a person who is tarred with the same brush as someone else is perceived as having the same faults as the other person being referred to. It's not clear why the expression took on this negative connotation, rather than just suggesting similarity or equality.

Spoon feeding

Spoon feeding is what you do with young children when they aren't capable of feeding themselves. In its figurative application. spoon feeding usually describes one of two types of people who don't act independently. The first group are those who are spoilt and pampered. in other words treated a bit like babies. The other group potentially suffer a slightly more sinister fate in that they are people who are brainwashed and prevented from thinking for themselves by being 'spoon fed' ideas and information that they consume without questioning.

Square meal

Yet another phrase with various possible origins. a 'square meal' is a hearty one. Some will tell you that the expression arose from the Royal Navy's practice of using square trays to serve the evening meal. which was the most substantial one of the of day. Others will assure you that the saying dates from medieval times. when food was served on trenchers – which originally were square-cut slices of stale brown bread. and later were made of wood.

It's just as likely. however. that the saying is in fact using an archaic meaning of the word 'square'. meaning 'proper. honest or straightforward'. That's certainly the sense of the word in the common phrase 'fair and square'. so it could equally apply here.

STALKING HORSE

Literally, this was a horse (real or a decoy) that a hunter would hide behind in order to get closer to their prey. In the nineteenth century the term began to be used in the political sense of something that allowed you to get closer to a goal, by meaning someone who was put forward to 'test the water' for another, and potentially more successful, candidate. In the UK in recent times, the expression has come to be used almost exclusively in leadership contests for political parties. The candidate in question has no realistic chance of winning the election, but his role is to gauge the weight of support for a challenge to the current leader and to reveal how well stronger candidates might fare in a leadership contest.

Stew in your own juice

If you're left to 'stew in your own juice' you're left alone to suffer your anger or disappointment, or to ponder the consequences of some sort of foolish action. 'Stewing', both culinary and metaphorical, involves a slow, simmering process, so by implication, you're left to it for quite some time. Presumably the outcome is meant to be ultimately a positive one, just as the finished stew would be!

Similarly, bubbling stew gave rise to the nineteenth-century expression 'in a stew', meaning to be in a state of anxiety.

Storm in a teacup

There are many versions of this saying, all conveying the sense of something blown out of proportion. There are international equivalents, such as the Dutch 'storm in a glass of water' and the rather unpleasant-sounding Hungarian variant 'tempest in a potty'. In the USA you're more likely to hear someone talking about a 'tempest in a teapot'.

The first use of a similar phrase dates back as far as the writing of Cicero, in 52 BC, which refers to 'whipping up waves in a ladle'. Shakespeare, of course, put it neatly too, in the title of one of his plays, when he called it Much Ado About Nothing.

SUN IS OVER the YARDARM

A naval expression. 'the sun is over the yardarm' means it's an appropriate time to have a drink. In the days of sailing ships. which did actually have a yardarm (the foreyard. the one nearest the bow in a square-rigged ship) the sun would rise over this around noon when the ship was in home waters. So presumably noon was deemed a suitable time to indulge in a 'little tipple'. These days. of course. the saying is used ironically more often than not and sometimes phrased in the form of a question – 'Is the sun over the yardarm?' – when you're asking if it's too early to have a drink.

Swing the lead

Aboard ship it used to be the task of the leadsman to find the depth of water in which his ship was sailing by casting a lead weight attached to a measuring line ahead of the vessel and noting how much line disappeared below the surface. It's thought that lazy leadsmen merely went through the motions by swinging the lead and that this, like many nautical expressions, has then come ashore as a term to describe shirking any activity by making up a plausible excuse or feigning illness.

In fact, it's also possible that this is a phrase that has been misheard or misunderstood. The leadsman was supervised, for one thing, and had to record all his findings, so he wouldn't have had a lot of opportunities to avoid his task. It's equally plausible, then, that this is a corruption of 'swing a leg' – meaning to pretend to be injured in order to get out of doing something. 'Swing a leg' was in fact used in both the army and navy in the sense of malingering, so it's a likely source of this corruption – even if the 'lead' version of the saying is the more common one today.

Take a dekko

From the Hindi verb dekhna, meaning to look at, we get our word for having a swift glance at something. It's one of many words that entered the English language from India in the nineteenth century when the British Army was stationed there, in the days when 'the sun never set' on the British Empire.

Take by storm

By the seventeenth century a 'storm' in English meant an assault of troops on a place and therefore somewhere 'taken by storm' was a position seized by a sudden and overwhelming attack. Now this former military term applies to anyone who becomes suddenly famous or popular – they take somewhere by storm when they achieve instant success or fame.

Take pot luck

If you're happy enough to eat whatever happens to be served up, then you're happy to take 'pot luck'. When most household cooking took place over an open fire the majority of meals were prepared in a large cooking pot that was kept boiling over the fire. This contained everything that was to be consumed in the meal: vegetables, cereals and, on occasion, a small amount of meat. With catering of this sort, a meal from the pot comprised whatever had been put into the pot to cook and 'taking pot luck' amounted to offering visitors the opportunity to join the family meal and share whatever happened to be in the pot at that time.

From the same source we get a 'pot luck' dinner or supper, which is a meal shared by a group of people who each bring a different dish. These days you can look up all sorts of rules on the 'etiquette' of such an occasion, but this seems to defeat the object and take the chance (and with it some of the fun) out of the event.

TAKE the BISCUIT

To 'take the biscuit' can be interpreted in two ways, depending whether it is being used ironically or not. In its most straightforward use, 'taking the biscuit' means being the best of the lot. However, it is often used ironically, in expressions like, 'I've heard some daft things in my time, but that takes the biscuit!'

'Taking the biscuit' is an Anglicised form of an expression common in America from the middle of the nineteenth century. The American expression refers to 'taking the cake', an allusion to the cake awarded to the winners of a 'cakewalk'. This was a nineteenth-century pastime, popular with African Americans, in which couples paraded arm in arm around a room. The couple judged to be the most graceful walkers 'took the cake' as their prize.

Take with a pinch of salt

Sometimes you'll hear 'a grain of salt' instead (from the Latin cum grano salis). but the meaning is the same – accept something up to a point. but remain slightly sceptical at the same time. Taking salt with food has for centuries been recommended to make it more palatable. and the figurative use arises from this.

Taken aback

If we're taken aback we're startled by something. The phrase suggests that. figuratively speaking. we have jumped back in surprise. This is yet another nautical expression that has come to be used on land – when a ship was taken aback its sails were being blown against the mast. preventing it from moving forward.

Talk turkey

This expression originated in America where it was in common usage by the middle of the nineteenth century. before spreading throughout the English-speaking world. 'Talking turkey' means 'talking business'. or 'talking seriously'. It appears to date from the early days of the colonies. when turkeys formed an important part of the trade between the Native Americans and the early settlers. Most trading meetings would involve the supplying of turkeys to the settlers and 'talking turkey' became a familiar saying whenever a colonist appeared to discuss business.

That's the way the cookie crumbles

The American 'cookie' takes its name from the Dutch 'koekje', meaning a little cake. 'That's the way the cookie crumbles' gained popularity after the Second World War as a fatalistic expression similar in meaning to 'what will be, will be', usually used when something turns out less promisingly that expected. It was used in many American advertisements in the 1950s, which increased its popularity as a saying, and is still used today on both sides of the Atlantic.

Cookies also feature in such phrases as 'smart cookie', a positive description of someone, and 'tough cookie', meaning someone awkward and unbending. In the USA you might also hear the description 'cookie-cutter' applied to something. This suggests that it lacks any originality or individuality, presumably because cookies shaped with a cookie cutter are all exactly the same.

Since the creation of the internet, of course, the word 'cookie' has acquired a whole new meaning, referring to data sent from a website to a user's browser. There are several theories about how the word came to be applied in this context, but like all the other associated new computer terminology, it's become a widely accepted term and is undoubtedly here to stay.

THREE SHEETS TO *the* WIND

This colourful naval expression for being very drunk dates from the days of sailing ships when sails were trimmed and set in their correct positions by means of ropes, known aboard ship as 'sheets'.

A sheet which had come loose, allowing part of the sail to flap freely, was said to be 'in the wind'. To be 'a sheet in the wind' then became naval slang for being slightly drunk – probably because of the association with being somewhat out of control. To be 'three sheets to (or in) the wind' was therefore far more serious and suggested that you really were 'pie-eyed' or had had 'a skinful'!

Throw the baby out with the bath water

This saying is a direct translation of a German proverb, and suggests that the essential elements of something can be lost through radical reform or rash change. It was known in England in the early years of the seventeenth century, even though taking a bath then was not an everyday experience.

Turn a blind eye

We've all done it – pretended not see something, or overlooked it to avoid any awkwardness. As a saying, this one has a fine pedigree and dates from the days when Britannia really did rule the waves. The year was 1801; the scene the battle of Copenhagen. Nelson, as second in command, was sent a signal (in the form of flags) by his superior Admiral Sir Hyde Parker, ordering him to disengage. However, he is reputed to have put his telescope to his blind eye and declared that he could not see the signal, telling his officers 'I have only one eye. I have the right to be blind sometimes.'

Turn-up for the books

Signifying a surprise or a stroke of good luck, this expression was originally 'a turn-up for the book'. The book in question was the one kept by a bookmaker, that is someone who took bets and kept a written record of them. A 'turn-up' was when an unbacked horse won. and therefore the bookmaker didn't have to pay out.

Upper crust

In days gone by loaves were baked directly on the floor of the oven. and consequently the lower part of the loaf became charred. This was cut off and fed to the menial domestic staff. while the top part. the 'upper crust' was offered to the most important guests. Figuratively it came to be a term for the aristocracy or higher echelons of society.

Upset the apple-cart

Meaning to cause upset. confusion or disruption. this phrase comes either from rural life or the wrestling ring. but 'the jury's out' as to which is the more likely.

The rural theory is of course a simple reference to an accident that could happen when harvested produce was piled high. The wrestling one relies on the suggestion that the 'apple-cart' meant the body. and upsetting the apple-cart became the colloquial term for a wrestling throw.

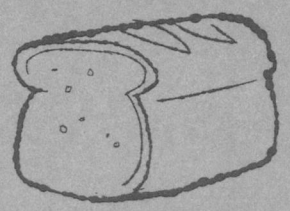

USE YOUR LOAF

In Cockney rhyming slang 'loaf of bread' means 'head'. As is usually the way with rhyming slang, the phrase is shortened simply to 'loaf' when it's used, and telling someone 'use your loaf' means 'use your head', or 'use your brains'.

Wet blanket

A 'wet blanket' is a person whose lack of enthusiasm spoils things for others, or who puts a figurative 'damper' on an idea. In literal form, of course, wet blankets actually have a very practical use, in smothering fires, but this idea of damping down has become the basis for a less than flattering description of a 'killjoy'.

When my ship comes in

Similar to 'when my numbers come up', this is a saying that conjures up the prospect of fortunes to come. In the days when most trading was done by merchant ships sailing around the world, waiting for your ship to come in was a tense time. Any number of things could go wrong and it was only when your ship landed safely back at shore, with the expected cargo safe and sound on board, that you could be certain that you had earned what you were expecting to and could pay your way.

Whistle for it

If you're hoping for something and someone tells you you can 'whistle for it', then the meaning is quite clear ~ you have no chance of getting it. Another saying from the days of sailing ships, this expression has its foundation in the belief that sailors could 'whistle up' a wind if their ship was becalmed. Whether this was based on a genuine optimism that it would work, or whether they really knew it was pointless (as suggested by the modern usage) isn't known.

Wild goose chase

This is not a wild chase after a goose (although the way we tend to say it suggests that it is), but a chase in the manner of a wild goose! Or more accurately – geese. The expression, meaning a useless or hopeless pursuit of something, derives from a sixteenth-century cross-country race on horseback. The game followed a sort of 'follow my leader' principle – so the riders, following one behind the other, resembled a flock of geese in flight.

With flying colours

Victorious warships signal their triumphs at sea by returning to port with all their 'colours', that is their flags, still flying. So anything accomplished 'with flying colours' can be regarded as a complete triumph, and more often than not the expression is used to signify passing some kind of test or exam.

Wouldn't say boo to a goose

In the sixteenth century, when geese were commonly reared, the expression 'he/she wouldn't say shoo to a goose' was coined to suggest that someone was very timid. Given that geese themselves are timid and could quite easily be shooed away, this suggests that the person in question is very unassertive, although it's true that geese can be quite noisy! At some point the phrase adopted the word 'boo' rather than 'shoo', and despite the fact that most people today wouldn't have any reason to be herding geese, it's still a common way to describe someone who is painfully shy.

Wouldn't touch it with a barge pole

Barge poles – used to propel canal boats or keep them from crashing into the bank – obviously have to be very long, and this expression refers to something that is so unpleasant that you wouldn't want to go near it. In the USA the phrase more often used was 'a ten-foot pole', which in fact was probably the same thing as a barge pole. Both of these sayings seem to have originated in the nineteenth century, and seem to be 'modernised' versions of a much earlier saying: 'wouldn't touch it with a pair of tongs'.

You can run, but you can't hide

In the world heavyweight boxing championship fight in the summer of 1946, Joe Louis was lined up against Billy Cotten. Cotten was known to be a fast mover, but Louis was unimpressed and warned 'He can run, but he can't hide.' When they met in the ring, Joe Louis's words proved to be true and he won the title with a knockout. The expression then passed into popular usage, but became rephrased into the form we know it today in the 1980s, when President Reagan warned terrorists who had hijacked an American airliner in Beirut, 'You can run, but you can't hide.'

You cannot be serious!

Anyone who watched even one tennis match in the 1980s will recognise this phrase. The trademark exclamation of American player John McEnroe, when questioning umpires' decisions in fiery outbursts, earned him the nickname 'Superbrat'. But the phrase caught on and today it is still widely used to express both real and mock incredulity.

You can't make an omelette without breaking eggs

This is a direct translation of a French saying and was originally intended as a warning to people that if you wanted results in some endeavour you had to put in the effort. As such, you'd think they could have come up with a metaphor concerning effort that was a bit more meaningful – after all, breaking eggs is pretty straightforward. These days, it's used more often in the wry sense that while you may be in a mess or a muddle, or very stressed, in the short term, you know it will be worth it in the long run, when you've achieved whatever it is you are trying to do.

YOU CAN'T TEACH AN OLD DOG NEW TRICKS

This proverb goes back at least as far as the sixteenth century and means that literally, the old have more trouble learning new things than the young, just as puppies can be trained quickly but older dogs are harder to teach. In its metaphorical sense with regard to people, it's also used to suggest that older people have more trouble taking on new ideas, and are set in their ways.